YOUTH AND DRUGS

Christian Heritage Rediscovered

The Series, as the name suggests, is meant to focus on Christian Faith & Living vis-à-vis topics like Literature & Poetry, Indigenous Philosophizing, Ethical response towards Agriculture, Health & Healing, Science & Technology, Eco-feminist Theology, Sociological approach towards Human Rights, Law & Politics, Arts, History of Ideas, Ancient Civilizations, Cultural Contiguity, Religious Cosmologies & Mysticism, Footsteps of famous Theologians, World Peace & Harmony, Global Capitalism, Network Marketing, Cybertheology, Population & Demographics, Epigraphic Studies, Contextualized Education, and many others. We welcome a Mss. on any topic/s mentioned, whether they are original works, scholarly monographs, collections of conference papers, revised dissertations, or translations of historical documents. Through the Series we, the Publishers, are striving to put forward published works that may help Institutions, Academic Bodies, Researchers, Scholars and the World at large in furthering their respective knowledge and understanding on the concerned subject. We welcome your comments on our efforts and further suggestions on how we can foster the upcoming thought provoking theologically grounded books.

Christian Heritage Rediscovered - 40

YOUTH AND DRUGS

Missional Concern Towards Therapeutic Care and Counselling

H. G. Mithra

CWI

Christian World Imprints™

First Published in 2016 by

Christian World Imprints(TM)
Christian Publishing & Books from India
H-12 Bali Nagar, **New Delhi-110015**
info@christianworldimprints.com
www.ChristianWorldImprints.com
Phone: +91 11 25465925

ISBN: 978-93-5148-141-6 (HB) ISBN: 978-93-5148-142-3 (PB)

Cataloging in Publication Data--DK
Courtesy: D.K. Agencies (P) Ltd. <docinfo@dkagencies.com>

Mithra, H. G., author.
Youth and drugs : missional concern towards therapeutic care and counselling / H.G. Mithra.
pages cm. -- (Christian heritage rediscovered ; 40)
Includes bibliographical references.
ISBN 9789351481416 (HB)
ISBN 9789351481423 (PB)

1. Youth--Drug use--India. 2. Youth--Drug use--Religious aspects--Christianity. I. Title. II. Series: Christian heritage rediscovered ; 40.

HV5824.Y68M58 2016 DDC 362.2908350954 23

Printed at D. K. Fine Art Press Pvt. Ltd.

Dedicated

to

My Parents & Friends

and

The Victims of Drug Abuse

Acknowledgements

This book is a by product of the research which was done nearly thirty years ago under the aegis of South Asia Institute of Advance Christian Studies at Bangalore in 1987-1988. As I was reading one day for some reference, I realized the value of this research and the material therein. That is when I thought of publishing it for the wider readership. I am glad Mr. Sudhanshu Kanda prevailed on me to publish something that would contribute to the fund of knowledge and that is how this work has come in print. Therefore, Christian World Imprints and its management are profusely thanked for bringing out this work.

I thank God for His intuition and prompting to take up this project which I hope will be of great help to those working with/ among the drug addicts and in rehabilitation centres in various parts of the country, particularly those Christian non-governmental organizations attached to Church Ministry and Mission.

I must thank SAIACS administration of those years, Dr. Graham Houghton and his team, the Library staff who were supportive in providing the required materials. Though SAIACS had limitations in more ways than one those days, yet it provided all possible help to carry out a quality research. When I walk back thirty years down the memory lane of my studies in poorly developed IV block Koramangala, it is unthinkable today to imagine that it was the same place where I did this initial work and got my degree. Now, it is called *Croremangala*, for it has become home for many software companies.

There is world of change I have not been to that place again, even if did, I may not recognize it today. It used to be called breeding ground for mosquitoes. Koramangala is transformed and one of the coveted/posh areas of Bangalore.

I must acknowledge the help that was given during this research by Dr. J. T. K. Daniel as a guide who went on to become Principal of Serampore College where I landed as professor after a decade. His insightful help and hospitality whenever I visited Madras Christian College to consult him is immensely appreciated. I did not have a copy of this research I did, with me for some reason; he gave me his copy when I called on him at Serampore in 1995.

I thank my pastor friend Rev. Michael Peppin who helped in proof reading and editing my research draft those days, though he is retired and I am reaching sixty, I wish to record my appreciation to him as well.

There are host of people who may have done something or the other during those days; I wish to acknowledge all those dear ones.

If it was not for keying in the whole text into the computer, it wouldn't be possible to add and to make corrections for the publication. The whole text was type written, unfortunately, I did not have the luxury of computers and they were rarely available for the public those days. SAIACS itself did not have one at that time. Today, SAIACS revolves around computerized world. I am told that they are the most modernized academic community in India today.

I owe a great deal of debt to my wife Irene who patiently took time to key into the computer so as to prepare this text for the publication. Without her help, it would not have been possible to bring this book out in print.

I wish to thank my daughters and wife for their sincere prayers and encouragement in getting this work done.

Dr. David C Scott, who was my teacher at BD did make a helpful suggestions during this research work in 1987. Those valuable suggestions are incorporated in this book.

Finally, I thank the Union Biblical Seminary and my student community here and elsewhere for their motivation and encouragement throughout my teaching ministry of 28 years. For some reasons, I did not take up publishing my works, I suppose there is time for everything and I am glad I was motivated to, at least now to get my thoughts in print.

I am grateful to God and my prayer partners here and everywhere for their constant friendship and motivation. I have gone through colourful experiences in life and they have taught lasting lessons to be a better teacher, preacher above all better human being. I have not finished learning and I continue to learn on the way of my life's journey till the end.

Preface

The United Nations recently declared India as southern Asia's biggest consumer of heroin, in a comprehensive drug report. Often thought of as an ideal transit point for countries like Afghanistan, Pakistan or Nepal, most of the drugs in southern Asia don't make it out of our country.

According to the Times of India, of the 40 tonnes of heroin produced in south Asia, nearly 17 tonnes are consumed in India. And with a trade value estimated to be $1.4 billion, heroin has become much more than a bad habit.

Of the 17 tonnes of heroin in India, about eight are of Afghan origin, and the other nine are indigenously manufactured. Unofficially, there are close to 5 million people addicted to heroin in India. And the rising student population in some southern and western cities account for much of the country's heroin use. [This information is collected from different internet sources].

Content in this book may appear ancient or outdated as one reads through but the challenge it poses to the mission and ministry today is as humongous as it was in 1980s and 1990s. In fact, this menace has come in different shades and colours affecting human beings particularly the younger generations. Such as mouth and lung cancers, ulcers, increased suicides, murders, road accidents due to drunken driving and drug effects, increase in smoking among the younger generations and offshoots of drug abuse like HIV and AIDS spread mainly by long distance driving force across India. Though we might like to wish away this menace as non-serious yet its ill effects are seen as serious as they appeared few decades ago. Part of India is still under the yoke of ill effects of drug abuse and its manifestations.

I have quoted recent newspaper article in this book elsewhere that the state of Punjab and its youth are the worst affected due to drug trafficking. As recently as January 19, 2016 *Times of India* Pune edition on page 9 quoted that 162-329 million drug abusers across the globe. Same paper on page 12 quoted: In 2014, the overdose death rate for whites aged 25-34 was five times its level in 1999, and the rate for 35-44 year old whites tripled during that period.

Times of India Pune edition of Friday, January 22, 2016 stated on page 5 that, Brown sugar worth 1.28 lakh (64 kg) has been seized from Vidya Jadav a woman drug peddler in Niradharnagar, Pimpri outskirts of Pune by the anti-narcotics cell.

Statistical inputs in this work has been duly updated according to the recent census and available global information for the present day readers.

Missional concerns of 1980s remain the same, if not increased interest among the Christian non-governmental organizations (NGOs). It may have solicited aggressive activities when it attacked humanity with its dreadful effects. There is in no doubt that focus and attention it got then may be missing but not its punch. Many scholars, psychologists, psychiatrists, medical personnel wrote and published their views as part of creating awareness of drug menace. Nowadays that is not seen as much as it was then since other pressing issues have got public's attention today. Drug abuse *per se* is not a new menace; it is still a killer factor of human lives.

The menace of drug abuse had swept all across the country in eighties among younger people particularly among the professional college students. Publicity it had got then was unprecedented. In fact this menace was indeed the fall out of 'hippy' culture in seventies and early eighties. Drug abuse had caught up with youngsters like wild fire. Worst cases were highlighted worst results of this menace were there for every,one to see.

Of course, our country is not new to the culture of drinking, smoking and abusing substances. Bhang drinking is part of festive celebration in Northern part of the country, consumption of rice bear is common in North-eastern region, and toddy consumption among toddy tappers in South India is known fact. Adulterated substance abuse to have higher kick became common among the younger generation.

In the context of such a scenario, author had done extensive research on this issue by visiting higher education Institutions, particularly Professional Colleges like Medical, Engineering, and Law. In these campuses students were experimenting with all kinds of combination of drugs. Hard core addict was practicing extreme measures like snake bite at tip of the toe or a tongue etc. Such cases were almost heading towards a slow death. This was reported and recorded in some of the reliable write ups. Terrifying experimentations were done by worst case.

First chapter of the book briefly describes various drugs that are abused among the students. It's mostly a theoretical in nature, scientific description of a drug and its bio-chemical effects, its origin and contemporary use of it.

Second chapter considers its worldwide network, where it is manufactured and how it is procured, who are involved in this clandestine business etc. Though, it is a dangerous yet it is one of the ways to become overnight rich and wealthy.

The ill effects of the dangerous business are discussed in chapter three. How society, religion and economics suffer due to this menace. What role do these agencies have in preventing its damaging effects on youth of this country?

Fourth chapter deals with Biblical and Ethical perspectives of drug abuse. What does Bible teach about life and its use and abuse? How should the youth who are victims of this menace be treated and rehabilitated? What ethical and moral responsibilities do the Church and the Society in general have in eradicating the life threatening addiction? Some of these questions are answered in this chapter.

Last chapter makes a general observations of the seriousness of the situation and the role of Church's mission and therapeutic care to those youth who have become a prey to the killer drugs either intentionally or unintentionally. Practical and therapeutic suggestions and recommendations are made to the general public, particularly Church for Missional and ministerial response to this invisible enemy of India. Nation must wake up from its slumber and act to save its name and fame.

Prof. H. G. Mithra
Union Biblical Seminary, Pune
April, 2016

Contents

Introduction

Drug addiction has become a major health problem in our country, and according to print media it is India`s enemy number One. Drug Abuse is prevalent among adolescents in high schools and colleges.[1] It is a destructive threat to the present and future generations and country's development and its future. Dr. Rajath Ray of the National Institute of Mental Health and Neuro Science (NIMHANS) said, "Drug abuse is and has always been very much a problem in India not merely confined to the West alone."[2] It is becoming or rather, has become, one of the most serious problems in the present day world. This worldwide problem is staggering, and it is a proven fact that in many countries a larger portion of crimes as well as many diseases are the outcome of alcoholism and drug addiction. It is increasing at an alarming rate in India today, despite the Narcotics Act 1986.

Drug abuse in India manifests at two levels in society. The traditional pattern found in rural India has existed for hundreds of years as has been discussed under the section Historical Survey of each category of drugs in this research work. It involves the use of bhang, charas, ganja and other products of the cannabis plant. In some areas like Rajasthan, Punjab, Uttar Pradesh, Madhya Pradesh and Assam, opium is also used.[3] This pattern of drug abuse is part of the lifestyle of the people to relax after a tiresome day's work, and this may be considered as a form of "controlled" drug abuse. It decreases the life expectancy and similarly decreases the work efficiency and general health. It is only a small number of cases where serious addiction, leading to major trauma and disruption of normal lifestyle occurs. As has been said earlier, the majority of such people live a normal life; take a small amount of drugs to relax after the day's work and on social occasions.

In the last decade, and particularly since 1980, a similar pattern of drug abuse has developed, predominantly among students in colleges and youth. The prevalent figures of drug abuse among students vary from 29.6 per cent to 56.2 per cent.[4] This pattern of abuse if not controlled results in a high proportion of addicts who often ruin their lives and careers.[5]

Drugs are destroying all the beautiful values of life and even leading to murder and suicide. Because drug use and abuse has biological, social, psychological, pharmacological, political, economic and spiritual implications.[6] Since, it has a multi-dimensional problem, it has to be viewed from more than one perspective. Further, drug abuse is symptomatic of individual, family and social stresses. Environment is as important as the individual in leading to drug abuse. Thus, it has become rampant and a serious threat to the families, institutions and society as a whole by its rapid spread to all sections of the society, especially in the major cities. So, it is estimated that at least one lakh, both young and old, have a drug problem in each of the major cities of Delhi, Mumbai and Kolkata, with thousands affected in other centres as well. According to the news report of the Deccan Herald, 16 May 1988, Mumbai alone had 1,20,000 heroin addicts,[7] claiming more children, many of them aged eleven to sixteen. A counsellor in Bangalore went so far as to reveal that even a six year old child was on drugs in the cantonment area.

What then is a drug? "A drug is any chemical substance that produces physical, mental, emotional or behavioural change in the user."[8] Perhaps drugs may be confined to what are called simples, balsams, balm gums, resins and exotic products used as medicaments in a dry state. Hence, the term drug can be traced back to the Dutch word, *droog*, meaning dry.[9] In a popular sense, the term drug refers mainly to a substance that effects psychological or behavioural functions and gradually leads to varying degrees of dependence.

There are many addiction-forming, mood-changing drugs, namely narcotics, hallucinogens, stimulants, depressants, hypnotics and tranquillisers. There are natural plant products such as opium and their derivatives, cannabis and others. Cocaine is one of the costliest and more powerful dependence-producing substances obtained from natural resources, thus it is called the **King of Drugs**. There are semi-synthetic and synthetic drugs which are produced in laboratories. Therefore, the first chapter in this book deals with drugs exclusively: their use and effect on human beings. The description, bio-chemical effects and symptoms that are produced by drug abuse, when and how a particular drug abused, to have [sic] euphoric feelings in the human history and the contemporary uses of drugs. These are the main topics discussed in the first chapter. However, it does not include alcohol and tobacco which are also drugs, because it is felt for various reasons that these subjects of alcoholism and tobacco smoking merits a separate discussion and wide research. This book is substance specific in its nature.

The second chapter in particular focuses its attention on the network of how drugs are acquired and distributed. It was a fascinating research, but on the other hand, it was dangerous to be involved in such research because it is a clandestine business. Information is not easily available due to strict vigilance. Each drug smuggler has his own helpers and highly skilled businessmen, specialised in distribution, packing and transporting. They hold strict confidence to the extent of losing one's life yet not revealing the secret of how they operate and who is their head for drug agency etc. Drug smugglers are wealthy people counting money in crores; they usually do not value life but money. So, one could say, for this very reason they are involved in destructive business such as drugs. *Times of India*, January 11, 2016 edition carried an article: "Hollywood star Sean Penn secretly met and interviewed Mexican *drug-lord* Joaquin Guzman Loera, known as 'El Chapo'".

From little children to the old all are involved, one way or the other, in this business. Rickshaw and taxi drivers, street vendors, betel-nut sellers, grocers, railway porters are chronic addicts. All these act as distribution points, selling drugs to make money and addicts to sustain their own habits. "Drugs are big business; strong political and economic interests are involved in the production, smuggling and distribution."[10] During electioneering as was reported in the newspapers of 1987 that in Gujarat and Rajasthan politicians offered marijuana to people and motivated them to vote for the party concerned. It is nothing but a kind of exploitation. Therefore, control of drug networks is extremely difficult. This chapter gives the basic idea as to where the sources of drugs are, how they come into society and what kinds of people are involved: such questions are answered with few illustrations. If this is to be stopped, there is a need for a strong national policy on narcotics and psychotropic drugs, as part of the national health policy. There has to be commitment to long-term action and a political will. Therefore, prolonged efforts are needed.

The third chapter deals with causative factors and the effects of drug abuse and addiction on society: the social, religious and economic aspects of life. Here, the responsibility of society is to make students feel accepted, important and needed in their service for making society better. Society is to fight and adapt preventive measures to eradicate the drug malady. Logically, this chapter explains the role of an individual who is a member of a family and a family is a unit of community and a society, so is the Church in society. It is interesting to note that an individual addict is not the only person suffering due to his indulgence in that dirty habit but the whole family suffers with him. Family religion is under question, and economy is drained. With regards to drug addiction, family alone will not suffer, but the neighbours suffer too. Because the freedom of children is curtailed, relationships with that suffering family are restrained and neighbours are in a dilemma and fear as to what will happen next to their children. Hence, this chapter encourages individuals and society, especially the Church, to play an important role to prevent the menace and protect the students. It also touches on how this drug business leads a country into economic imbalance and morally it cripples the nation. The consequences of drug abuse are very severe, resulting in incurable diseases like

AIDS (Acquired Immune Deficiency Syndrome), STD (Sexually Transmitted Diseases), prostitution, homosexuality, impotency, mental retardation among young lives, crime, robbery and so many other unfortunate happenings.[11] It is nothing but contagious spreading rapidly among college students, victimising every college student in India today. Indeed it is horrifying. Murder, suicide and death are the ultimate ends of drug addiction. Thus, this chapter addresses an individual as a person and a citizen of the country, a family a unit, community a part of society and a church a religious body to strive to fight against gigantic empire the drug menace in one's own respective place as they spot and sense its spread.

The fourth chapter is an important one because it gives a clear picture of man and the purpose of human's life and its excitation, euphoria, merrymaking is not the sole meaning of human existence. But God has a definite plan and purpose for human's life on earth. One has to realize the vitality and preciousness of life and the moral and ethical domains of his own religion and society.

Having known this truth about human beings, why do our young students go astray? Maybe due to a need of belonging, to overcome fear and rejection, alter mood and escape from the unpleasant realities of life or it may simply be due to curiosity and fun. In order to be accepted by their peer groups, students go in for these destructive habits. A person's youth can be one of the happiest stages of life but the changing standards of this world and its problems have robbed their happiness. One of these changing standards is drug circulation and free availability is creating confusion and chaos in our college campuses, hostels, on the streets and at home. It has turned many homes into a place of mourning; hundreds of lives are threatened and deprived of their bright future. It is precisely in this situation that the love of Christ can be made manifest. Christian counsellors and trained workers can convey this by their attitudes to the extent that their own lives have been influenced by Christ. It is exactly for such as these Christ died on Calvary.

The final chapter is exclusively optimistic in the approach to drug abusers or addicts. God, who created them and us, is concerned, and cares for each one and comes in search of all of us that He might restore us to His fellowship. God is a missionary God, even to the drug abusers/addicts. They are to be accepted, treated as any sick person, and given the needed care and love, thereby bringing them back to a civilization that they are precious in the sight of God and are created in His image. If God's intention is to seek and to save addicts, so is to be the Church's concern. As Christians, committed to the cause of Christ, we ought to be involved in creating an awareness among people that the drugs are not the answer to the problems they face, but Christ is the answer to loneliness, dejection, frustrations, hopelessness and failure. Therefore, the Church's immediate mission field ought to be the works of drug addicts. The Church, being God's agent for change on earth, must be on the frontline to fight against this menace. The Church has to become a channel of restoration, rehabilitation and de-addiction centre to the addict.

However, rehabilitation of drug abusers and addiction has various facets, no one person can be involved in all of them, each stage is fairly specialised. The author feels that he is called to bring this issue to the surface to rouse an awareness of the people especially committed Christians, victims, government agencies, non-government organizations, etc., so our concerted effort would be made to eradicate the problem. It is like that of William Carey who published two magazines to create an awareness on various aspects, including *sati*, which indeed resulted positively in due course of time, as we all know, from the history of our country.[12] The author hopes to create this kind of awareness to save young students for whom his ministry stands committed. This research is done to conscientize the Church, Society and Nations to take the issue seriously and thereby prevent drug menace. For, "after all, the youth of a nation are the trustees of posterity."[13] Of course, one cannot purchase health. As a broken pot cannot be reassembled, so is health. Certainly drug addiction is sinful in the sense that it enslaves men and women and denies God's purpose for their lives. God's concern is to save every sinner including an addict; hence drug abuse must become a serious concern for each Christian worker as it is to his Creator. Christian families and parents are being devastated as they see their children's lives are ruined by drug addiction. The productive, happy future, foreseen for their children is turning into despair and hope turning to heartbreak. Therefore, this research which is turned into a book for the wider readership explains the multiplicity of factors which have caused the drug problem and exhorts every Christian and citizen to be involved in one way or another to prevent drug abuse among college students and save their future.

The methodology applied in this research is socio-analytical and empirical which includes socio-economic factors, library research, interviews, personal talks, newspapers, official documents, government personnel, students, college students, mass media and rehabilitated addicts. The identity of those interviewed is not revealed for obvious reasons.

This research is not an exhaustive one, but it is a humble endeavour to conscientize people with Biblical and ethical perspective to fight the battle of drug menace. The earnest desire of the writer is that people would go through this material and know what is happening in the world and in their neighbourhood. The problem is at our doorsteps, let us awake and say no to the drug world. The mind is not damaged by addiction, but skin infections, liver complaints, wasted muscles, blood diseases, unhealthy bowel habits and aching limbs are the results. So let us arise, and save such students of our land for Christ's sake fulfilling the mission and ministry of Christ in our times.

End Notes

1. "The Editorial Speaks," *Health Action*, Vol. 1, No. 11, November 1988, p. 1.
2. Kenneth J. Lawson (ed), *The Christian Response to Alcohol and Drug Problem* (Bangalore: Ecumenical Christian Centre, 1983), p. 1.
3. Michael O'Toole, *Drugs and Youth in India* (Goa: The OM Yeshu Niketan Society, 1987), p. 6.
4. Lawton, *The Christian*, p. 6.
5. O'Toole, *Drugs*, p. 4.
6. "Addiction: Churches Responsibilities," *The South India Churchman*, August 1988, p. 3.
7. "More Heroin Addicts ..." Deccan Herald. 14 May 1988, p. viii.

8. "Drugs," Don Bosco Youth Animation - Bangalore (leaflet in another's possession).
9. K. L. Kaufman, *The World Book of Encyclopedia*, s.v. "Drugs".
10. "The Editorial. *Health Action*. P.3.
11. "AIDS: A Scientific and Christian Perspective," *Light of Life*, April 1988, p. 12.
12. Interview with Suri Williams, Sri Lanka, Y.F.C. Area Director, Bangalore on 12 June 1988.
13. N. F. Fernandes (ed), *Indian Youth Care*, Vol. 1, No. 1, August 1986, p. 4.

Chapter 1

Drugs
Use and Abuse

The drug menace was unknown in the history of India, but today, it is rampant and this issue is discussed in this chapter.

I. DEPRESSANTS

Many regular kind of people have used various types of drugs known as, depressants. They are used to make people relaxed and tranquil. Hence, they are sometimes called, tranquillisers, or sedatives. They calm down mentally or physically disturbed persons and are therefore also called, downers. They may be given by doctors for certain illness, but they can also be taken in such a way as to be harmful. This gives way to abuse. In fact this is the way drug abuse can occur.[1] Depressants have the potential for abuse associated with both psychological and physiological dependence. They are prescribed by physicians as well as psychiatrists for relief from anxiety, tension, irritability, and for the treatment of insomnia. In excessive amount, they produce a state of intoxication that is remarkably similar to that of alcohol. These drugs are used to allay mental states characterised by anxiety, tension and hyperactivity. This generation seeks a merry life and nothing else;

whereas life is not always a bed of roses. Since they want to run away from problems, tensions and worries of life, they seek depressants to enable them to cope with life. These drugs are consumed by many people working in call centres, film industry and mining.

Scientific Description of the Drug

Barbiturates: a type of depressant tablet which contains chemicals called Barbiturates; they are often contained in sleeping pills. These are often dangerous than other depressants or downers because an overdose leads to death. Barbiturates are derived from Barbituric acid, which is formed from malonic acid and urea. Later sedatives were formed by adding various chemical groups. There are following kinds of barbiturates a) long-acting 6-14 hours, luminal; b). intermediate 3-4 hours; c) ultra-short – under 3 hours. Intermediate and ultra-short barbiturates are dangerous, the latter produces anaesthesia within a minute after intravenous administration.[2] It is estimated by the medical authorities that there are some one thousand five hundred types of barbiturates available, but all are legally restricted to prescription use only.[3] Some barbiturates are used for epilepsy and intravenous anaesthesia, but also an anti-convulsant. However, barbiturates are poisonous and addictive. The use of stimulant drugs in conjunction with supportive measures is not accepted.

Bio-chemical Effects and Symptoms

Barbiturate abusers and addicts are generally emotionally maladjusted persons. A small dose gives relaxation, but a heavy dose causes sluggishness and depression. At times a user may go into a coma: it also leads to defective speech, poor comprehension, impaired memory, confusion in problem-solving and decision-making. Strong doses produce sleep immediately. They can cause severe poisoning, deep coma and, as said earlier, respiratory and kidney failure and death.

Primary Effects: Regular users are gloomy and quarrelsome, have impaired memory and depression.

Side Effects: Habit-forming and physically addictive, withdrawal is both painful and dangerous. Serious accidents can occur since warning signals of pain are effectively dulled.

Symptoms: Appearance of drunkenness, slurred speech, mental and emotional instability, burns on fingers, hair-trigger, temper, insomnia, weakness, nausea, vomiting, abdominal cramps, rapid heart rate, elevated blood pressure, and loss of weight. The symptoms usually exhibit themselves for about a week.[4]

Historical Survey of the Use of the Drug in Indian Society

Barbital was manufactured in 1883 and was the first among barbiturates to be used in medicine. It was manufactured as veronal. Barbiturates were first used in 1903. Over two thousand five hundred barbiturates have been produced but only fifty commercial brands are now available and only twelve are widely used.[5] It is very difficult to date its flow into Indian society. But its use is generally understood to have been abused in the last few decades in India, especially among college students both male and female. It is not so much in use as other drugs in India.

Contemporary Use of the Drug

The Indian Youth Care Journal records a million addicts in the USA. With over three thousand deaths every year, due to overdoses of barbiturates.[6] And it has led many to suicide. It is very much abused among medical and engineering students of India and Europe. Since it is the sleep inducer, students take this to avoid the problems of life. Excessive use leads to physiological and psychological dependence. These barbiturates are available in India for a variable price from rupees 5/- for ten tablets to rupees 8/- for ten tablets. They are taken orally as a tablet or capsule and can also be injected. They are more dangerous than other depressants. Quite a few suicidal cases are from the users of this drug. Withdrawal from heavy barbiturates can result in serious convulsions therefore withdrawal needs careful control and supervision.[7]

Users' secret names of barbiturates are blue angel, blue bird, blue heavens, tips, candy, Christmas rolls, dolls, golf ball, downs, bombs, beans, green, idiot pills, Mexican reds, peanuts, pink ladies, rainbows, reds, red devils, softball, tools, yellow and yellow jackets etc.

Methagulone: A chemical containing mandrax, a very common tablet. It is abused by young people in India. This chemical is also found in other tablets. Mandrax tablets are no longer made legally because their use is being abused. Illegal manufacturer of mandrax in India has given rise to major illegal export of these drugs as India is major international source for it. This may be linked to the fact that mandrax was first prepared in India in 1952.[8] Early part of year, 1988, lakhs of rupees worth of mandrax tablets were seized by Intelligence officers in Mumbai.[9]

Mepsobamate: This was first synthesised in 1950. It introduced the era of mild or minor tranquillisers.

Benzodiazepines: Family of depressants, relieves anxiety, tensions, and muscle spasms, produces sedations and prevents convulsion. This drug is easily available to young people whose parents may be using them and leaving them around carelessly. All of these are abused and most of these relieve tension and anxiety but also cause psychological and physiological dependence. [Most of the medical terms of drugs are taken from *Encyclopaedia of Britannica – Macropedia*].

II. HALLUCINOGENS

Hallucinogens are psychomimetic drugs which produce such psychotic reactions as depression, mania or schizophrenia in normal persons. Those that produce schizophrenic reactions are termed hallucinogens. Hallucinogen drugs both natural and synthetic produce changes in perception which vary from sensory illusions to outright hallucinations. "Illusions are mere distortions of what is sensed while hallucinations are objects where there are, in fact, none to be sensed."[10] They induce a state of excitation of the central nervous system (CNS) manifested by alterations of mood, usually euphoric, but sometimes severely depressive, which gives rise to the possibility of suicide. The most common danger is that hallucinogens are unpredictable in their effect. Each time they are consumed, under their influence the sense of direction, distance and time, become disoriented. Thus the user may say, "I see sounds and hear colours."[11] Larger amounts of the drug produce delusions and visual hallucinations. Hallucinogens are also known as psychedelic drugs, i.e., one's that enrich the mind and enlarge the vision.

The users will be uniquely sensitive at the time of use. The commonly abused drugs in this family are mescaline, psilocybin, psilocin, lysergic acid diethylamide (LSD) and phencyclidine (PCP). The primary effect of this major classification of natural and synthetic drugs is to distort the senses and produce hallucinatory experiences: experiences which depart from reality.

Scientific Description of the Drug

LSD: It is an abbreviation of the German for Lysergic acid Diethylamide.[12] It is the most mind alerting of chemicals and is an odourless white powder. It is produced in laboratories. LSD is not widely produced in India, most of it comes from illegal laboratories abroad.[13] It is stored in small –plastic bags, which are square in shape. This dried solution can be licked, sucked or dissolved to take it. Sometimes LSD is sold as tiny pills called, microdots, or pyramids.[14] LSD is derived mainly from an infected grain with fungus ergot. It contains ergot alkaloids, a bitter plant origin too. LSD is the street name of a semi-synthetic derivative of an ergot fungus of Rye, a substance that grows on grain.[15]

Bio-chemical Effects and Symptoms

Only a tiny amount of this drug is required to give an experience known as trip, which may last for hours, or even days, says a recovered addict in Bangalore. Sometimes, if adulterated with emphetamines, it can result in a bad trip. Compared to western youth; LSD is less used among Indian students.

Primary Effects: This family of drugs cause, hallucinations, nervous breakdowns, mental disturbances, unusual love for nature and environment, ability to discriminate between facts and fantasy, intensification of sensory perception. The addict speaks of seeing sounds and tasting colours and smelling noises.

Side Effects: The LSD trip may not always be a pleasurable experience. It would well turn out to be a horrifying and traumatic experience. If taken by a maladjusted and mentally ill person. It may lead to violent and dangerous behaviour. Because the user sometimes imagines he is being persecuted by people. In order to defend himself he will not hesitate to attack anyone he comes across. Therefore, the person dependant on LSD is dangerous to himself and to society in general.

The prolonged use of LSD may damage the brain, cause deformity or mental retardation in the user's offspring. It also causes psychotic behaviour, suicidal tendencies and mental abnormality. If women take LSD during pregnancy, there can be incidents of miscarriage or deformity in a newborn baby, because the drug action is chiefly in the brain or nervous system. However, it is not toxic and rarely produces addiction or withdrawal symptoms even after long use. Hallucinogens trips seldom last longer than four or five hours, after which the tripper passes into sleep.[16]

Symptoms: Signs of drug intoxication, emotional shifting moods, frequently, laughing or crying uncontrollably, not easy to communicate with LSD user, dark glasses, often even worn in the night. The user spends hours together deeply engrossed in admiring plants, flowers, and other beauties of nature and may feel he understands the truth and secret of creation now.[17]

Historical Survey of the Use of this Drug in Indian Society

Dr. Albert Hoffmann discovered this drug in 1938 to be one of the most mind-alerting chemicals. "In the early 1960s, in the USA those who experimented with LSD paid glowing tributes to its capacity to enable the user to discover and put to use his latent talents and potential hitherto undetected."[18] It has been found in the city of

Bangalore only a few drug abusers go in for LSD since it has good and bad trips. However, among the medical and engineering students today, it is very prevalent for the very reason it expands the mind and leads to self-improvement. Moreover all hallucinogens are relatively non-toxic and no deaths have been reported so far.

Contemporary Use of the Drug

It is very prevalent among Indian College students as of today's trend, for the simple reason it is believed to expand the mind and enlarge the vision by increasing sensory awareness. It helps one to escape from realities of life which involve a fight against day-to-day anxieties and frustrations. It also leads to self-improvement, to a greater personal insight and better understanding and appreciation of human being and nature.[19] *The National Institute of Drug abuse India Research Journal* (NIDA), estimates that 22,41,000 people used LSD occasionally in 1977 in the USA. This is usually taken orally; effects begin in an hour and last for 2 to 12 hours.

Modern students' name for LSD: animal, beast, barrels, blue-chairs, cap, chief, cubs "D' dot, flash, ghost, peace, pure, love, purple heart, squirrel, tabs, ticket, wedding bells, sunshine, zen and so on. Other hallucinogens are mescaline, phencyclidine (PCI), psilocybin and psilocyn.

Mescaline: It is manufactured out of the head or buttons of the peyote cactus, an alkaloid with hallucinogenic properties. It is less potent than LSD. Its effects appear after use in two to three hours, and last for four to twelve hours. Peyote is a small cactus native to Mexico and Texas. It was employed by Indians in northern Mexico as a part of religious rites. Mescaline also can be produced synthetically. A dose of 350-500mg produces illusions and hallucinations. The Native American Church legally uses peyote; it is limited to *bona fide* members of the Church only.[20]

Psilocybin and Psilocyn: Like Peyote Cactus, psilocybe mushrooms have been used for centuries. When eaten these mushrooms, it affect a person's mood and perception in a manner similar to mescaline and LSD, their active ingredients psilocybin and psilocyn are chemically related to LSD. It is not much in use among students of India in comparison to other drugs.

Psencylidine (PCP) was investigated upon in the 1950s as a human anaesthetic but because of side effects of confusion and delirium or disordered state of mind with incoherent speech and hallucinations its development for human use was discontinued. Today most, if not all, PCP available in the illicit market is produced in clandestine laboratories.

This drug, popularly known as PCP, is sold under various names including angel dust, supergrass, crystal, and rocket fuel. It is also often misrepresented as mescaline, LSD, and tetra-hydrocannabinol (THC). Its effects on human beings are, the user feels a sense of detachment, distance and estrangement from his/her surroundings. Numbness, slurred speech, a blank stare, rapid and involuntary eye movements and a exaggerated gait or manner of walking are commonly observable effects and symptoms. Severe mood disorders, acute anxiety occurs. PCP poses a greater risk to the user than any other drugs of abuse.[21]

Because of its adverse effects, it is now used medically, only for veterinary purpose. It can be inhaled, swallowed or smoked often in conjunction with Marijuana.

III. NARCOTICS

The word, narcotic, comes from a Greek word, neckosis - numbing. This type of drug medically usually refers to any drug that dulls a person's senses and when taken in small doses produce a sense of well being. This term was used loosely in the Nineteenth Century for all non-alcoholic drugs. Schultes defined Narcotics as "any substance that has depressive effect, whether high or great, on the central nervous system.[22] Narcotic refers to Opium and its derivatives or synthetic substitutes. It is one of the oldest drug classifications known to mankind. It relieves pain, stops cough and diarrhoea. There are three types of narcotics: a) Natural origins b) semi synthetic, and c) synthetic. The term also assumed a social meaning that encompassed debility or feebleness, addiction, insanity, crime and death. Also any illicit drug is referred to as a narcotic. But in terms of pharmacological effects, it should be used only to refer to the analgesic depressant opium, the opiates and the opioids.[23]

The main source of natural narcotics, poppypapaver is believed to have grown in the Mediterranean region as early as 300 BC. Now it is cultivated around the world including Hungary, Yugoslavia, Turkey, Burma, Thailand, Vietnam, Pakistan, Afghanistan, Iran, China, Mexico and India.[24] The milky fluid that oozes from incisions in the unripe seed pod is taken out and dried in the air to produce opium gum. The extract may be in liquid, solid or powder forms.[25] Therefore, anyone who is connected with non-medicinal use of this drug is considered to be a degenerate or a criminal.

(i) Narcotics of Natural Origin

There are mainly three types of Narcotics of Natural Origin: Opium, Morphine and Codeine

Scientific Description of the Drug

Opium is derived from the poppy plant, which is cultivated in India mainly in the states of Uttar Pradesh, Madhya Pradesh and Rajasthan. The milky fluid that oozes from incisions in the unripe seed pod has since ancient times been scraped by hand and air-dried to produce opium gum. Fresh opium is a chestnut-brown gummy substance. If preserved it becomes hard, brittle and dark brownish, almost black in colour and bitter in taste.[26] This is of a narcotic origin from which all the opiates are derived, eg., Morphine, codeine, alkaloids. At least twenty-five alkaloids are extracted from opium.

Bio-chemical Effects and Symptoms

Opium users are characterised by attitudes of pessimism and futility which lead to aggressive or violent behaviour. An addict is prone to crime, to steal in order to meet the expenses of the drug also, if he is an employee he becomes an undependable employee due to the opium effect on his central nervous system. The regular use of opium produces drug tolerance, also a psychological and physiological dependence upon the drug. An opium user usually passes rapidly into the narcotic state without any prior excitement. Drowsiness yields to sleep and coma, which ends in death due to the failure of respiration. Clues to find in an adult addict is the comatose patent has a cold and clammy skin, livid lips and ear tips, and pinpoint pupils. The heart's action may be feeble, the pulse irregular and slow

Historical Survey of the Use of the Drug in Indian Society

The word, opium, comes from the Greek, opion, juice and was first used for therapeutic purposes. The earliest known reference to it is in Assyrian medical tablets under the term *arat pa, pa-a* possible origin for the Latin, papaver. It is also designated by the Summerian Ideogram, *hul, gil,* which dates from the Fourth Millennium B.C. and signifies joy, hul, and plant, gil, indicating that the Summerians were familiar with the euphoric properties. Later references are found in the Ebers Egyptian papyri about 1550 BC which mentions opium among approximately seven hundred remedies. Greek and Roman medical writers referred to the drug about the year 40 AD. It is believed that Arab traders carried opium to India before the time of Mohammed (570-632 AD) but its use there was doubtless spread by the Mohammedan invasions. In 1781, the East India Company took the trade into their hands. At present, the most important producing countries are Persia, India, China , Russia, Turkestan, Afghanistan and Turkey.[27] Opium was used to treat fifty different diseases. In the seventeenth century it was praised as God's gift to humanity to relieve suffering in England.[28] Opium was a therapeutic agent until the Twentieth century. But today it is the most abused drug among students, according to those who were interviewed. Also it is abused by slum dwellers and poor people since it was available at licensed shops until 1947.[29]

Contemporary Use of the Drug

Natural origin narcotics use and abuse in India has become the number one enemy of society. It is sold secretly in all the streets of major cities in India. Opium smoking is a habit of millions in the Orient. Opium and cannabis are the principal drugs of abuse in India. Narcotic drugs are being sold and circulated more in the Cantonment and Fraser town areas said the Police Commissioner of Bangalore city, in a seminar conducted by the Organisation called HOPE, at Malleswaram. This drug is used worldwide. In 1977, the USA had 43, 49,000 opiate users.[30] It is also said that in 1914, there were 1,50,000 narcotic addicts in the USA: women outnumbered the men. After ten years of the Harrison Narcotics Act 1914, a Public Health Survey showed 1,10,000 addicts, one out of every one thousand of the general population.[31]

The *Times of India* (a daily newspaper) said that rupees 11 lakh worth of opium was seized on 23 May 1988 in Bangalore at Banswadi by the Narcotics Control Bureau (NCB) of South Zone; it was contraband from Rajasthan which was to be sent to Trichy in Tamilnadu and from there to Sri Lanka. The Director of NCB, R. V. Kumar, Bangalore, said India has become a major centre for smuggling opium from areas of the Golden Crescent to Europe, Australia, Sri Lanka and Singapore. He also said that Pakistan is the major producer and exporter of opium.[32] The October issue of the Illustrated weekly, 1988, records that Mr. Dalbir Singh, Deputy Director General NCB has been responsible for the destruction of opium crops in about one hundred acres of land in Dehra Dun district during 1987 to 1988.[33] This drug is being used in many Indian villages after tiresome work, but it is being abused among Engineering and Medical college students of Bangalore in a high percentage, as well as in other major cities of India.

Slang names: chandu, medak, ope, haffine.

Morphine: The principal constituent of opium, it is one of the most effective drugs known for the relief of pain.[34] It was separated in 1803, and named after *Morpheus* the Greek god of dreams.[35] Claude Bernard, the renowned physiologist of the late Nineteenth Century was the first one to use morphine on animals.[36] It is odourless, tastes bitter, and is administered by injection below the skin which is called skin popping, intramuscularly or intravenously. The latter method is the one most frequently resorted to by the addicts.[37] It relieves pain and induces sleep. This drug was used widely on troops during the Civil war. It was also used to relieve pain in childbirth for many years. Morphine develops psychological and physiological dependence on the drug within a matter of a few days. However, some consider this to be superior to all other pain relievers. Today heroin has replaced both opium and morphine as drugs used by the youth.[38]

Slang names: Cube, emm, firatline, monkey, morphy, pink, sweet jesus, uncle, upper, white, nurse.

Codeine: It is produced from morphine, is used for moderate relief in the form of asprine; it is also injected. And it is also used for the relief of cough, in the form of syrups.[39] Compared to morphine, it produces less analgesia and sedation. Codeine is a natural opiate.[40]

(ii) Semi-Synthetic Narcotics

There are two most popular semi-synthetic narcotics, Heroin and Brown sugar.

Scientific Description of the Drug

Heroin is made in the laboratory from morphine. It is many times stronger than morphine both in the good feeling it produces and in the addiction it causes.[41] Pure heroin is a white powder with a bitter taste. Illicitly produced heroin varies in colour from white to brown because of impurities left from the manufacturing process.

Brown sugar is the residue resulting from the chemical reaction by which morphine is converted to heroin. It is the street and slang name for heroin, says an addict. Since the pure heroin produced in the laboratory is quite expensive, about rupees 400 for a gram, Brown sugar so called because it is adulterated by adding diluents such as sugar, starch, powdered milk and other powders.[42] Brown sugar also contains certain chemicals and catalysts (e.g. zinc) which are required for the chemical reactions. Pure heroin is refined and therefore costly, and is rarely available on the streets for addicts. Brown sugar contains impurities and so is much cheaper as expensive purification process is avoided. Heroin is equated with brown sugar and, in some places, it is accepted as heroin in either form.[43] In recent years, the police have located heroin laboratories around Delhi, said the Government official at Bangalore.[44] In other words, brown sugar is a crude form of heroin.

Bio-chemical Effects and Symptoms

The first try may result in an unpleasant trip, which results in vomiting, feelings of sickness and disappointment. However, from the second taste onwards the individual does begin to experience the pleasurable effects – a high, with relaxed and pleasant feelings of euphoria. As the effect begins to wear off, a regular user begins to experience an increasing urge for more of the drug.[45] Tolerance develops rapidly and regular use, for a few days is sufficient to produce a psychological and physiological dependence on the drug.

Primary Effects: A few seconds after injection, the addicts face flushes and he/she gets the feeling that everything is fine and right. He/she begins to indulge in day dreams. He/she experiences a short euphoric spasm, followed by a high, and a feeling of relaxation. Heroin trips take the addict roaring high into a make-believe world of his own. Heroin is also used as a powerful pain killer. In addition to lessening the feeling of pain, it also decreases the awareness of the user to his surroundings, the addict's pupils become constricted and he feels a tingling sensation, particularly in the abdomen.

Side Effects: Judgement, self-control and attention rapidly deteriorate, mental degeneration, loss of weight and appetite: lead to convulsions and, finally, death. Withdrawal is painful and dangerous. Addicts usually resort to crime to support their habit.

High intensity of drug leads the addict to beg, borrow, steal or even kill, if need be, to secure the means to satisfy his craving. It is not, therefore, surprising to hear if female addicts hire out their bodies to any bidder in exchange for a few rupees. Today this has led many girls into prostitution and made them into streetwalkers.

Once the craving for the drug sets in, it does not matter what time it is, with whom he is, or where he is, whether in a temple, church or mosque, in the school or in a college, in the bus, train or plane. At a wedding or at a funeral; at home or anywhere in the world; if the thought of taking the drug becomes uppermost and predominant in his mind, the addicts put aside everything else as secondary[46]

In certain cases, it leads an addict to insanity and impotency. Cases of this drug need strict supervision and care because brown sugar, if neglected, will ultimately lead to a terrible death. Clues to spot brown sugar addicts are: constricted pupils, severe chills, sweating, watery eyes, and running noses: restless tossing whether asleep or awake, white needle scars or reddish scab on arms and thighs; users are dazed and often begin staring into space dreamily.[47]

Historical Survey of the Use of the Drug in Indian Society

Heroin was isolated in 1898 in Germany, by the pharmacologist Heinrich Dresser in search for non-habit forming analgesics (which produces relief from pain) to take the place of morphine.[48] It was first synthesised from morphine in 1874. Heroin was not used extensively in medicine until the beginning of this century. But the Bayer Company in Germany first started commercial production of the new pain remedy in 1898 as is mentioned above. Since about 1985, an adulterated form of heroin has become widely available in India, especially in the cities and among the student population.[49]

Heroin is believed to have got its name from the German, *hero-isch*, meaning large, big or powerful, most potent.[50] This drug was ushered in a new era in the history of our country that may appropriately be described as the Drug Age.[51] Due to the heavy demand, the composition of brown sugar is available at nook and corner of our major cities, at *pan-bidi* shops, grocery shops, outside schools, colleges, restaurants and theatres, near bus stops and railway stations. The network has rapidly made inroads into the district and taluka levels too.[52]

Contemporary Use of the Drug

Until about the beginning of the 1980s, heroin was considered a luxury. Even today, it appears beyond common man's reach. Internet sources searched on 23.01.2016, stated a gram of Heroin in Brunei costs $1330.4, in New Zealand it is sold at $717.4, US $200, UAE $165, Australia $500, Bangladesh $125 per gram. Interestingly in India it is sold at very cheap rate compared to the above rates $10.93 per gram, where as Nepal pays $64 per gram [information is collected from Havoc Scope – Global Black Market]. Therefore, only used by affluent urban families because the price of a kilo of heroin of ninety per cent purity in Pakistan was worth rupees 40,000 (Indian rupees, in 1987). As it crosses the border, the price shoots up to rupees 80,000; on reaching European markets, notably Frankfurt, it rockets to a staggering rupees 300 lakhs per kilo in 1987.[53] The value of pure Heroin has gone up by ten to hundred percent in some countries. Hence, it began to be concocted with several other substances, such as iodine, arsenic, *chuna*, rat-poison, *dhatura*, lactose, *agarbathi* ash, crushed amphetamines and barbiturates – even crushed glass to give weight. It is marketed in plastic vials or vessels especially designed for holding liquid medicines, as also in powder form. Prior to the Narcotics Drugs and Psychotropic substances Act 1985, the street price per vial was around rupees 7 to 8. After the amendment of the law, however, the price doubled to around rupees 15 per vial, says Benjamin Lobo, an experienced dependent on drugs.

India had become a transit city, today it is a user city, with five lakh people addicted to heroin and brown sugar.[54] On 8 May 1988, the *Times of India* said that the number of heroin addicts in India had reached the seven lakh mark and 70% of the addicts in the city hailed from the lower strata of society. This menace was not heard of in Indian history, the number of brown sugar addicts is increasing rapidly day-by-day. "The day is not far off when every school child will have been offered brown sugar at least once in his or her school years," says Mr. A N Veera Raghvan of Mumbai.[55] Our country is becoming (has become) a key consumer of narcotics ranging from heroin to methaqualone. Heroin seizures in India spurted from 200 kg in 1984 to 2,900 kgs in 1987.[56] Specially about a couple of years ago, Mumbai had about eighty thousand brown sugar addicts. Now there are more than one lakh twenty thousand in that city alone.[57]

The American *TIME* magazine quoted, "some of the latest abusers are barely out of babyhood."[58] But it is not new in India because recently at Bangalore an eleven, and a six year old girl were hooked on brown sugar and one had become a streetwalker. The contemporary use of the drug is severe in every part of the country today and the Narcotics Control Board is fighting against the number one enemy of India.

Brown sugar is usually smoked, chased or injected. It cannot be ingested orally, since oral ingestion does not produce the desired trips, thus the stuff has got to be smoked, chased or fixed if the user is to derive any pleasurable experience. If taken by mouth it would only serve to cause ulcers, jaundice, liver cirrhosis, rash and other medical complications, hence addicts smoke it. A little tobacco is removed from a cigarette and the balance loosened, The desired quantum of the drug is then poured into the cigarette and made to sink deep into the level of the filter. The joined portion of the cigarette paper is usually wetted with spittle so as to ensure a longer smoke, says the recovered addict. It is also chased, i.e. the substance is placed on a strip of aluminium foil (the silver wrapping in cigarette packets) and the foil is heated from below, using a candle or matchstick. The heated substance liquefies and rolls along the foil emanating blackish fumes. These fumes are inhaled, using a long hollow tube known as a chaser, about 3' long. The fumes are, so to say chased by using the chaser and hence, the name.[59] Fixing/injecting mainlining is taking the drug directly into the blood stream. The drug is dissolved in a few drops of sour lime and plain tap water in a spoon. The solution is then heated, drawn into a syringe and injected intravenously, this is called, in drug abusers' terms, fixing.

Slang names: balloon, bigbag, berry , boy, brown sugar, gard, chip, hero, hallen, horse, 'H', junk, Jones, pure, salt, garbage, snack, Old Steve.[60]

(iii) Synthetic Narcotics

This category includes Pethidine and Methadone which are produced entirely within the laboratory. Penthidine is widely used to relieve moderate to severe pain. Methadone was synthesized by German scientists due to the shortage of morphine during World War II. It is widely used in the treatment of narcotic addicts. These drugs are taken orally and intravenously by addicts and an overdose leads to death. These too are dangerous drugs.

IV. STIMULANTS

The major classification of drugs that stimulate the Central Nervous System (CNS) in contrast to the depressants which slow down the activity of the CNS. They excite functional activity in the body, alertness and so on.[61] The two prevalently used stimulants are nicotine and caffeine. When used in moderation, these stimulants tend to relieve fatigue and increase alertness.

There are however, more potent stimulants like cocaine and the amphetamines that have high dependence. Stimulant users report to the use of these drugs for their euphoric effects – to feel more active, stronger, more decisive and self possessed. Because of the cumulative effects of these drugs chronic users may take stimulants in the morning and depressants in the evening in order to induce sleep. This pattern usually causes psychological and physiological illnesses.[62]

If withdrawn, chronic users exhibit profound depression, apathy, fatigue and disturbed sleep. If they continue for weeks, then suicidal tendencies may develop. Some scientists have said that these are not addictive but habit forming drugs and are commonly used.

This category of drugs include Amphetamine and Cocaine.

Scientific Description of the Drug

Amphetamine is one of the series of synthetic drugs with pronounced stimulatory actions on the Central Nervous System. It is a colourless, mobile, slowly volatile liquid with an acrid (bitterly pungent) taste, a slight odour of geranium (herb) leaves. The most widely used one is amphetamine sulphate, a white odourless powder with a slightly numbing and bitter taste.[63] Amphetamines are prescribed by physicians chiefly to reduce appetite in obese patients. Amphetamines are concocted compounds of organic base. The most common stimulants in India contain chemicals known as emphetamines. The brand name best known is Dexedrine.[64] These are available in tablet form. The drugs of this group have the advantage of being relatively non-toxic, addiction to them is rare, and there are no serious ill effects.

Bio-chemical Effects and Symptoms

Normal doses produce wakefulness, increased alertness and initiatives and great deal of anxiety, induces elations and elevation of mood; a sense of euphoria, increased talkativeness and ability to concentrate; the person feels confident and pleasant. However, the conspicuous effects are drowsiness, mental depression and reduced ability to concentrate.[65]

Amphetamines have been shown to enhance performance in humans in various tests; Particularly at the end of test-period, when boredom and irritation would have otherwise decreased performance. "Several compounds belonging to the amphetamine series have been used for their *anorexigenic* properties for weight reducing purposes."[66] It has been reported to increase libido and sexual pleasure, particularly in women. In men, high doses may increase libido but sometimes it causes impotency. Blood pressure and heart in man are affected by the use of amphetamine. The rate and depth of respiration are increased with moderate and large amphetamine doses.

An overdose leads to over-stimulation and restlessness, inability to sleep, tremor, irritability. Abdominal cramping with nausea, vomiting and diarrhoea may also occur; it can also produce loss of consciousness, collapse and death. These are undesirable effects on human beings.[67]

How to spot the addicts: the clues are dilation of pupils, a common sign in intoxication where high doses have been employed. The user may also exhibit symptoms of paranoid schizophrenia; at this stage users may be inclined to be violent. Also an addict susceptible to such ailments as pneumonia and brain damage.[68]

Historical Survey of the Use of the Drug in Indian Society

Amphetamine was first prepared in 1887 by Edeleano and Methylanyphetamine in 1919 by Ogats in Japan. The first pharmacological studies were by Alles in 1927. In 1931, amphetamine was introduced as a nasal decongestant in the form of the benezedrine inhaler. It was used for the treatment of narcolepsy in 1935 and of depression in 1936.[69]

As early as 1938 it was realized that misuse of amphetamine could bring about a psychotic condition. But in the 1950s there was some abuse, by 1953 certainly, among college students. However, in India, amphetamine is mixed with other substances and there are not many amphetamine dependants in India. It was at some time in the 1970s introduced to the world of youth. College students take this drug in order to have a thrill, or a high. They think it helps them to study before examinations. "After the stimulating effects of the drug wear off what follow is a come-down period of exhaustion and depression."[70]

Contemporary Use of the Drug

Initially, **Amphetamines** were considered to be the wonder drug, pep pills helped people temporarily to function above their normal capacity. It was widely used by soldiers during world war II to overcome fatigue by night-shift workers, long distance truck drivers, students cramming for their examinations, athletes, as also housewives, pilots and astronauts on long term mission.[71] This drug is used in the morning and the depressants to induct sleep in the night. Cases of this nature may lead to chronic disease and death.

It is inhaled, injected intravenously, orally taken as tablets, or in capsule form. They are available at about rupees 10 per twenty-five tablets but in the black market cost rupees 100 per twenty-five tablets.[72]

Slang names: 'A', Bam, Bena, Bennier, black beauty, black bird, bottles, browns, chalk, chicken, power, Xmas trees, co-pilots, crossroads, crystal, diet pills, double cross, fives, football, French blue, hearts, horse, heads, in -betweens, jam, jelly babies, jolly beans, jugs, lepers, oranges, pep pills, roses, speed, sweets, turkey, truck drivers, ups and whites.

Cocaine: is the most potent stimulant of natural origin. Cocaine is extracted from the leaves of the coca plant which belongs to the family of the *erythroxylaceae* plant. This grows to a height of 8 feet. It thrives best in hot climates. The leaves have a tea-like odour; when chewed they produce a sense of warmth in the mouth and have a pleasant pungent taste.[73] It grows in south America, cocaine is in the form of salt, a white fluffy powder that resembles crystalline snow. Occasionally, it is made into a pill.

The only medical use of cocaine is based on its ability to interrupt conduction in the nerves, thus producing local anaesthesia, especially of the mucous membranes of the eye, nose and throat. "The first use of its local anaesthetic action was made in Vienna in 1884."[74]

It was isolated in 1857 by Albert Niemann. It was hailed by many as a wonder drug. Sigmund Freud recommended its use for the treatment of morphine and alcohol dependence, asthma, digestive disorders, depression and fatigue. It is also used as a nerve-blocking agent.[75] Cocaine is very costly, the street value in India is between rupees 1200 to rupees 1800 per gram and it is known as the **King of Drugs**.[76] It is therefore diluted at each level of distribution. Cocaine precipitates a sense of wellbeing for four to six hours duration; it gives a feeling of peace and contentment. Cocaine induces sleeplessness and excitement; stimulates and accentuates the sexual process. It also induces remarkable overconfidence in one's ability and physical strength.

A large does can cause depression and exhaustion, lasting for many days, even convulsions and death due to paralysis of the respiratory centre; damage of the nasal membrane caused by snoring, severe weight loss. Vitamin deficiencies are caused, especially Vitamin A, B2, C and E, Calcium, iron, iodine, phosphorus, magnesium and zinc.[77] Addicts are often fearful and may suffer from the paranoiac belief of being threatened. They are dangerous and commonly carry weapons, which they are likely to use. Finally they end up in mental hospitals. *TIME* magazine of 30 May 1987 recorded,

> Kids who sell the crack because divorce has caused widows to work hard,
> It has made an impact on kids in the family where children try to relieve,
> Their mother's suffering, they sell crack in order to be breadwinners,
> Earning rupees 600 a week.[78]

Symptoms: dilated pupils, loss of a sense of time, fully alert, seems perceptive, physical reactions are sharp and rise in temperature.

NIDA research issue recorded 59, 53,000 cocaine users in 1985 of thc cighteen to twenty-five years of age group in the USA. *The Illustrated Weekly of India* of 23 October 1987, records cocaine seizure by the Indian Narcotics Control Bureau in Delhi and Mumbai. Cocaine is taken orally in a powder form and is kept below the tongue, or it is taken with betel leaves but addicts usually snort, or, sniff it for heightened effect. It is also injected directly into the bloodstream. If mixed with heroin it can be smoked. The smoking of cocaine originated in Peru during the early 1970s.[79]

Slang names: Big C, Blow, birdie, Bernice, came, Charlie, colas, coke, flake, snow, dream-dust, girl, gold dust, her, ice, lady, mosquito, paradise, crack, sugar, white girl, white horse, wings and witch.

Other stimulants are: dextro-amphetamine, methamphetamine, methedrine, caffeine and narcotics, some of which are mentioned earlier.

V. CANNABIS

Cannabis is one of the types of drugs known to humanity for years, especially in traditional Indian and religious ceremonial use. Cannabis is the Latin for hemp, drugs derived from the botanical plant class of the same name, cannabis. Both cannabis and Marijuana are interchangeably used to refer to all intoxicating properties. Marijuana is only the name used in the West for Cannabis productions or properties.

Botanists Richard E Schultz at Harvard University and Loran C Anderson at Florida State University proved scientifically that there are three kinds of Cannabis:

a. Cannabis – sativa
b. Cannabis – indica
c. Cannabis – ruderalis [80]

Cannabis Sativa grows upto eighteen feet, thrives in cool and damp climates. It grows wild throughout most of the tropics and in temperate regions of the world. It has got seven leaflets which are narrow. "It contains four hundred different substances."[81] Cannabis-Indica grows upto 3 and a half to 4 feet, thrives in a hot and dry climate and has nine broad leaflets. Cannabis Ruderalis grows upto1 to 2 and a half feet, never branches, is found primarily in Russia and has three leaflets of an oval or elliptic form. All these contain Delta 9-Hydrocannabinol (THC) Cannabis Indica has the most and Cannabis Ruderalis has the least. Sativa can be used as an animal feed also to produce oil to cook and in making paint. Tetrehydro Cannabinol a psycho-active alkaloid of the cannabis plant was first synthesized in 1965. Out of this plant, marijuana, a leaf-dust, is produced and hashish or *charas* is a blackish small ball that is a concentrated form of Marijuana. Hashish has twenty per cent of THC and Hash Oil has forty per cent THC. A pure THC is very expensive to produce. It is only used for research purposes. Around the mid Nineteenth Century it was thought to be effective in treating a wide range of physical and mental ailments. After the arrival of new synthetic drugs in the market in the twentieth century, interest in Cannabis production, as a medication, waned.[82]

The effects of cannabis resemble those of LSD and depressants, partially. Cannabis is cultivated all over India and it, too is abused. However, prolonged use may cause tolerance as also a psychological dependence. Some scientists have said it will not produce physiological dependence.

Scientific Description of the Drug

Hashish: The Cannabis plant has leaves, flowers, resin, seeds, stem and roots. All are significant in the preparation of the drug in a form that is used. A number of such preparations are extracts of the active drug THC.[83]

Hashish or *Charas* is made from the resin-rich parts of the plant and the method of preparation varies from region to region. It has quite a high content of the active drug THC. It varies in colour from brown to black, often with a greenish tinge, it is semi-solid (resembles animal dung) and is easily rolled into small balls, large amounts are sold as bricks, or slabs, or cakes.

Bio-chemical Effects and Symptoms

Cannabis has been used as a folk medicine in the east for hundreds of years. It is, reported, the Chinese emperor of about 3000 BC recommended hemp products to treat female weaknesses, rheumatism, malaria, *beri beri*, constipation and absent-mindedness. In India it was used to treat gastro-intestinal complaints and catarrh, also as a nerve stimulant.[84]

Effects of Cannabis: feeling of happiness, excitement and disassociation of ideas, errors in time and space, enhancement of senses, especially of hearing, fixed idea of delusions, and damage to emotions, irresistible impulses; illusions and hallucinations. The effects are dose-related.[85] It is also claimed to give relaxation and peace, an enhanced appreciation of music and colour, heightened awareness of self and reality. It is said to make one feel good and bring one into closer relationship with things and people.[86] It also causes fear and panic, poor memory, mental disturbances like unstable personality, lethargy, triggers sexual debauchery and crime.

Physical Effects: liver damage, chromosome damage or genetic defects: brain damage discovered by Bristol research workers, cancer reported by Dr. B. F. Cain, Director of the Auckland Cancer Research Laboratory. He said burning of hashish products polyclic aromatic hydrocarbons have repeatedly shown capable of producing cancer in experimental animals.

Symptoms: lethargy is the key. Many college students have agreed about this that it makes them lazy, dropouts, due to hashish use, magical thinking, lots of ideas and do nothing about this.

Historical Survey of Use of the Drug in Indian Society

Cannabis, or Indian hemp, has been known to man for some five thousand years. Originally its fibres were converted into rope and textiles. Later it began to be used in the practice of medicine and as an anaesthetic in surgery by the Chinese, Hindu and Arab physicians. There are references to its use as an intoxicant by the Assyrians around 650 BC. The spread of the cannabis drug became incorporated into the Hindu religion and the hemp plant was thought to possess divine properties. This drug is known in India as bhang, in the West Indies as *ganga*, *kif*, in Morocco, marijuana in the USA and UK. Its resin is known as hashish in Arabia and *Charas* in India. The word, marijuana, seems to have come from the Mexican-Spanish mariguana, or the Portuguese, mariquango, meaning intoxicant.87 This is the oldest drug in Indian culture and society.

Contemporary Use of the Drug

Cannabis is being used all over the world under varied names and trade names. In Indian villages, people take it in the evening to get relaxation after a tiresome day's work. But college students use it for kicks, or thrills. Interviews show that most of the professional college students of Bangalore use marijuana extensively next to heroin because it is cheap and easily available. Russel Market's backstreets are pretty famous for selling *ganja* or cannabis leaves. *NIDA* sponsored national survey of 1979 indicated that in the USA, 68.2% young adults in the age group of 18 to 25; 30.9% youth of 12 to 17; 19.6% adults of 26 and above were using marijuana.

In India, its circulation is wide. *The Times of India* of 13 June 1988 says 14 crores worth of *charas* was seized in Delhi on 12 June 1988.88 In Kerala and Tamilnadu, about 1,100 acres of the cannabis crop was destroyed under the supervision of Dalbir Singh, Deputy Director General of NCB of India. Over 160 kg of *ganja* was seized by Jogendra Singh, Deputy Director, Varanasi; and 4,565 kg hashish was seized by R. N. Kakar, Deputy Director, Mumbai, at Talasari about 150 km. from Mumbai.89 And, 1,743 kg. Hashish was seized by J. S. R. Khating, Deputy Director of Calcutta during the same year. This simply shows the danger that our country is facing and heading towards. If preventive measures are not taken, the whole of India will become a consumer country. Cannabis products are usually smoked in an emptied cigarette or *chillum* or water pipe; it is also sold in the form of tablets. Sometimes it is mixed with tobacco and smoked occasionally; it can be eaten mixed with honey. It is rarely applied with butter and eaten; and it can also be made into candy and chewed.[90]

Slang names: aeroplane, atom bomb, aunt Mary, baby, bar, boo, bhang, brick, bush, can, charge, churus, cocktail, fatty, ding, duby, finger, flowers, gates, Ghana, gold, grass, herb, hotsticks, Indian boy, Jane, Kif, Lobo, Log, Mo, mother Numberpin, pot, reefer, rope, sweet lucy, weed, wheat, root, hashish, hash, *charas,* dynamite, black-Russian, half-moon, quarter moon and soles, *ganga* and *ganja*.

There are other drugs called Inhalants which are inhaled or sniffed, such as glues, aerosole, spray paints, lighter fluid, and gasoline. S.T.P. (Serenity, tranquillity and peace) were first synthesised by Dow Chemical Company, a notorious underground chemist who stole the formula and introduced it to the public. STP produced intense hallucinations lasting from four to twenty-two hours,[91] Dimethyl Tryptamine (DMT) is a naturally synthesised hallucinogen. Ritalin is a synthetic central stimulant, taken by mouth or injected. Catnip is a mild stimulant, khat a modest stimulant, kava a mild intoxicant with sedative effects. Nutmeg is similar to mescaline and is an excitant and stimulant.[92]

Apart from the drugs that are mentioned, there are unconventional abuses. Addicts in Mumbai may graduate to the chronic abuse of brown sugar, or even postgraduate to snakebites, which are available at prices ranging from rupees 10 to rupees 75 per bite. The favourite, however, seems to be the one available at rupees 40. Cots are provided for the addicts to lie upon, while the snake man merrily makes his rounds with the snake in hand (about 1 and half feet in hand) administering the bites. The site for the bite is usually between the fingers or toes, as the addict may desire. For a more intense high, the tip of the tongue is exposed to the snake. The effects last for twenty-four to thirty-six hours. A scorpion sting administered in like manner is available at a cheaper rate. It is obvious that chronics, who have ceased to obtain the desired high from other drugs, resort to this dreadful abuse. One more fascinating or horrifying tale of the chronic brown sugar addict is about the one who inhaled the fumes from a lizard's skin to have a kick, because he could not get money to buy brown sugar.[93] However, this kind of unconventional abuse has not been disclosed in Bangalore. This is the fate of India today.

End Notes

1. Michael O'Toole, *Drugs and Youth in India* (Goa: The Om Yeshu Niketan Society, 1987), p. 16
2. Benjamin P Lobo, *The Answer to Drug Addiction* (Bombay : Joseph Fernandes Printers, 1986), p. 60
3. Debhora Glory, "Random Notes on Drugs," Seminar paper at Union Biblical Seminary, Pune, 1986, p. 17.
4. Lobo, *Drug Addiction*, p. 61.
5. Jacke Nelson, *National Institute on Drug Abuse, Research Technology*, Issue No.16, s.v. Barbiturates.
6. N. F. Fernandes (ed*). Indian Youth Care*, Vol. No. 3, November 1986, p. 6
7. Yusuf A Merchant, *Brown Sugar Addiction* (Bombay: St Marthoma Church Day Care Centres, 1987), p. 172.
8. O'Toole, *Drugs and Youth*, p. 16.
9. Sailesh Kottary, "Busting the Mob," *Illustrated Weekly* October 23, 1988, Vol. CIX, No. 43, October, 1988, p. 11.
10. *Encyclopedia Britannica, Macropedia*, s.v. "Drugs and Drug Addiction".
11. Lobo, *Drug Addition*, p. 66.
12. *Ibid.*, p. 67.
13. O'Toole, *Drugs and Youth*, p. 21.
14. *Ibid.*
15. Merchant, *Brown Sugar*, p. 175.
16. n.a., "Can Drug Addiction be cured," *Mirror,* April 1988, p. 22.
17. Lobo, *Drug Addiction*, p. 68.
18. *Ibid.*, p. 67.
19. *Ibid.*, p. 68.

20. Nelson (ed.), *National Institute on Drug Abuse (India) Research Journal,* Issue no. 29, p. 60.
21. Lobo, *Drug Addiction*, p. 69.
22. Nelson, *NIDA*. Issue no. 26, 64.
23. *Ibid.*
24. Lobo, *Drug Addiction,* p. 52.
25. *Ibid.*
26. *Ibid.*
27. *Encyclopaedia of the Social Sciences*. s.v. "Drug Addiction," by C. E. Terry.
28. Nelson, *NIDA*. Issue 26, s.v. "Opium".
29. Kenneth J Lawton (ed.) *The Christian Response to Alcohol and Drug Problem* (Bangalore : Ecunemical Christian Cente, 1983). p. 1.
30. Louire G Richard, *NIDA*. Research Monograph Series, No. 35, p. 63.
31. *Encyclopaedia Americans*, s.v. "Drug" by Austin S.
32. n.a., "Rs.11 lakh worth opium..." *The Times of India*, 24 May 1988, p. 3 (Daily newspaper from Bangalore).
33. Kottary, "Busting the Mob," p. 11.
34. Lobo, *Drug Addiction*, p. 53.
35. Nelson, *NIDA*, Issue no. 26. s.v. "Morphine"
36. *Britannica*. s.v. "Drugs and Drug Addiction."
37. Lobo, *Drug Addiction*, p. 53.
38. O'Toole, *Drugs and Youth*, p. 23.
39. Lobo, *Drug Addiction*, p. 54.
40. Nelson, *NIDA*, no. 26, s.v. "Codeine."
41. O'Toole, *Drugs and Youth*, p. 24
42. Lobo, *Drug Addiction*. p. 54
43. O'Toole, *Drugs and Youth*, p. 24
44. Interview with a Government official, Police Commissioner's Office, Bangalore, Karnataka on 24 November 1988.
45. Lobo, *Drug Addiction*. p. 54.
46. *Ibid.*, p. 30.
47. Debbora, "Random Notes," p. 18.
48. Nelson, *NIDA*, 26, s.v. "Heroin."
49. O'Toole , *Drugs and Youth*, p. 24.
50. Nelson, *NIDA* , 26, s.v. "Heroin."
51. Lobo, *Drug Addiction*, p. 17.
52. *Ibid.*
53. *Ibid.*, p.15.
54. Merchant, *Brown Sugar*, back cover page.
55. "Kick that Habit." *The Times of India*, Bangalore, 8 May 1988.
56. "Narcotic Haul," *The Times of India*, Bangalore, 9 May 1988, p. 8.
57. "Give me little Gard," *Blitz*, 22 August 1987, p. 19.

58. "Narcotics," *The Times of India*, 9 May 1988, p. 8.
59. Lobo, *Drug Addiction*. pp. 55-56.
60. Nelson, *NIDA*: 26, s.v. "Brown Sugar."
61. *Ibid.*, s.v. "Stimulants."
62. Lobo, *Drug Addiction*, p. 63.
63. *Encyclopaedia of Britannica*, Vol. 1. s.v. "Amphetamine," by John C Bellin,
64. William R Martin, *Drug Addiction II* (Berlin: Springer Verlag, 1977), p. 248.
65. O'Toole, *Drugs and Youth*, p. 18.
66. Martin, *Drug Addiction* II, p. 230.
67. *Britannica,* Vol. I. s.v. "Amphetamine," by John C Bu.
68. Debbora, "Random Notes," p. 17.
69. Kenneth Leech, *A Practical Guide to the Drug Scene* (London: Sheldon Press, 1974), p. 12.
70. Peter Hardman and Eric Jay, *Probe to Drug* (London: SCM Ptrdd, 1969), p.11.
71. Lobo, *Drug Addiction*, p. 65.
72. Merchant, *Brown Sugar*, p. 172.
73. *Britannica*, Vol.5, s.v. "Cocaine."
74. *Ibid.*
75. Nelson, *NIDA* : 26. s.v. "Cocaine,"
76. Merchant, *Brown Sugar*, p. 179.
77. *Ibid.*, p. 181.
78. "Kids who sell the Crack," *TIME,* 30 May 1988.
79. Nelson, *NIDA :* 26, s.v. "Cocaine."
80. *Ibid.*, s.v. "Cannabis."
81. Merchant, *Brown Sugar*, p. 182.
82. Lobo, *Drug Addiction*, p. 70.
83. O'Toole, *Drugs and Youth*, p. 11.
84. D. R. Copestake, *Cannabis: is Hash Safe* (Exeter: The Paternoster Press, 1979), p. 15.
85. Martin, *Addiction* II, p. 384.
86. Copestake, *Cannabis*, p. 15.
87. Leech, *A Practical Guide*, p. 35.
88. "14 Crore worth Charas Seized." *Times of India*, Bangalore: 12 June 1988.
89. Kottary, "Busting the Mob," p. 11.
90. Debbora, "Random Notes," p. 13.
91. Donald B Louria, *Overcoming Drugs* (New York: McGraw Hill Company, 1971, p. 219.
92. *Ibid.*, pp. 224-226.
93. Lobo, *Drug Addiction*, p. 73.

Chapter 2

Networking
Acquisition and Distribution

In the light of what has been discussed in the previous chapter about drugs and its effects, now it is interesting as well as intriguing to investigate and to study the means and methods of acquiring and distributing drugs unlawfully in India. The reason for this statement is that the people about whom society is least concerned, and the things or articles which people do not view with suspicion are in fact the people and things that are used as a means of distribution; such as, tins of well known brands of pure ghee, well-dressed official-like people, garbage picking children, playing children in the street, prostitutes, shopkeepers, businessmen, tourists, young college students, street vendors, chocolate wrappers, and so many other things. People, in society as a whole, are usually not sceptical about the above-mentioned persons or articles, yet it is true of Indian society today that they are the means by which drugs are unlawfully distributed.

Source of Drugs

The dethronement of the Shah of Iran and the troubled situation in Afghanistan at the beginning of this decade, brought about a lull in the drug traffic to the USA and Europe, so drug traffickers in the Golden Crescent looked towards India as a transit zone to channel tons of lethal heroin to the USA and European cities.[1] It is said a transit city will always become a consumer city in course of time; this has happened in the case of India. In fact, in Mumbai, heroin was known as "Iranian Gard,"[2] since it comes from the Golden Crescent.

From Outside the City

Apart from opium and marijuana, other such drugs are imported: mainly from the Golden Crescent and the Golden Triangle. Dalbir Singh, Deputy Director General of NCB says,

> What we are facing is actually a transit problem as more than 90% of the heroin is from the Golden Crescent region comprising of Afghanistan, Iran, and Turkey. The traditional north-eastern over Land routes to Europe were disrupted due to the region becoming a theatre of warfare between Iran and Iraq and the Soviet occupation Afghanistan. Hence, the supply routes have been moved south-eastwards, into Pakistan and on to the plains of India.[3]

There are experts who constitute the major Indian Narcotics Traffickers. Some of them are arrested by the Narcotics Control Bureau of India, and some are not. They are big businessmen who are well trained and well informed about the Narcotic Control Bureau. The major drug-running syndicates and drug smugglers shuttle from one place to another. The more the Indian Narcotics Control Bureau seizes contraband drugs, the more its inflow increases because by the time the NCB investigates one method of the drug-running syndicate, the syndicate has already changed to a completely new method. So, country which is producing narcotics will openly say that it does so.

In fact, it will flatly deny such an accusation. Pakistan is said to be the main place for producing heroin and other narcotics. In other words, it is the major producer and exporter of opium.[4] Kenneth Lawton, in his paper, "Drug Problem: A World View," says

> Crimes not known before have come with foreign workers and the eroding of old legal controls. There is now an illegal production of 40,000 tons of cannabis and 1,500 tons of illegal and illicit opium per year. The main sources having moved from the Golden Triangle to the Golden Crescent.[5]

Most of the synthetic drugs come from outside the country, especially those that are produced in the laboratories. This Golden Triangle comprises of Burma, Thailand, Laos and South East Africa. These countries have been the main sources of supply of illicit heroin and other drugs of abuse, but in recent years, the Golden Crescent comprising of Pakistan, Afghanistan, Turkey and Iran have taken over as a leading supplier to the world. It is estimated that seventy percent of the world's heroin hails from this place.[6]

So then, the bare worldview tells us that the semi-synthetic and synthetic drugs of abuse are poured into one or more major city of India and from thence. They are channelized to all the major cities of the country.

It has been discussed so far how drugs are poured into the country and then into the major cities. A Government official of the NCB said that Delhi and Mumbai are the leading transit cities for contraband drugs and they are also major consumer cities – having over a lakh addicts in each of them. These cities have spread the dangerous disease of drug taking to almost all the major cities in India. Now it is reaching district and *taluka* levels of every state in India.

According to Government officials, there are about fifty thousand addicts in Bangalore. Users and abusers are countless, especially in colleges. It was very clear from the interviews conducted in professional colleges that almost every second student is an abuser or user, but very few are addicts. How do they sustain their habit of drugs? In reality most of the narcotics and psychotropic substances are imported into the city. Here is the police official's statement:

Statement of Cases booked by the Special Squad
Under the Narcotic Drugs and Psychotropic Substances
Act, during 1987, up to 31.10.1987

Name of the Drug	No. of Cases	No. of Persons	Qty. of Drug Seized
Brown Sugar	21	30	120 Kgs.
Ganja	51	63	21 Kgs.

Rupees 11 lakhs worth of opium was seized on the 23 May, 1988 in Bangalore, at Banaswadi, by the NCB, South Zone.[8]

Everything that has been said in the preceding paragraphs is connected with tracing the original drug spring from which drugs are spread all over through various channels. The city gets them from the country and the country gets them from the other producing countries like Pakistan, Afghanistan, Iran, Turkey and so many other countries. The point to bring out here is to show that the consumer city may not necessarily be the producer city. However, production of drugs in India cannot be ruled out since in and around Delhi there are laboratories which produce synthetic and semi-synthetic drugs. Mumbai too produces them, as has been mentioned earlier. The question is not how much is produced but how it is acquired.

Manufactured in the City

According to the survey and research done by the Government officials there is no drug production in Bangalore city because of tight vigilance of the special squad. Marijuana is grown everywhere in small quantities in backyards of houses, in the middle or corners of gardens. Even in small flower pots and occasionally in the fields. No synthetic or semi-synthetic drugs are available illegally in some pharmaceutical shop according to a rehabilitated abuser.[9]

Bangalore has become one of the user and abuser cities because of modernity and fascination that the drug world has brought in.

Marijuana is not an addictive drug commonly known among the abusers; therefore it is tested by every single student in the professional and non-professional colleges. There are around one hundred and eight colleges in Bangalore, of which about eighty to ninety per cent are users: forty to fifty per cent abusers: and twenty to thirty-five per cent addicts: said Mr. 'A' an Engineering student.[10]

Most drugs are not manufactured in and around Bangalore city as has been said earlier. They are brought in from the outside. However, there may be several small laboratories which supply semi-synthetic drugs to the abusers. Here is the case of an addict: "one day I ran out of hard drugs, so I went around waking up friends on the campus, but I did not get the stuff I wanted. I asked my friend whether he could drive me to a house in the city since I was not in a position to drive myself. He agreed and we went along to the spot. There I met two young Muslim men whom I knew to be connected with drug dealings. They smiled and called me closer, and asked how much I needed. I told them and they gave it to me, at that odd hour, and said I am welcome any time. "We are producing our own," they said."[11] This is only a synopsis of the story that was narrated. The person concerned was a medical student in one of the colleges in Bangalore. It clearly shows that hard drugs are being made in this city in small quantities, but they have not yet been captured by the police because people who are indulging in this kind of business are skilled and intelligent. They are fully alert and always on the watch: therefore, it is not easy to catch or arrest them. They have highly trained couriers and are aware of Government officials' movements and activities in and around their area. No officials can make out who is passing information, how it is done, and so on. No one knows actually, except an odd drug abuser or an addict, and the manufacturer. Most often a drug addict is kept in the dark about where the drug is produced, etc., the reasons being that an addict is not a reliable and dependable person. He/she can utter anything when he is on a high. Therefore, he is not told anything; only the needed stuff is supplied to him: not any other information.

Sometimes the hard drugs are bought by agents and adulterated in order to make a larger profit; many diluents are added to the pure form of any drug, especially heroin.

Whether manufactured, or brought in from different places, it is available mostly in a few parts of Bangalore in lump sum amounts, places like Lingarajapuram, Banswadi, Cantonment, Fraser Town, Jayanagar and other places where a particular community of people are in the majority.[12] However, it cannot be localised to those few places because the papers, police officials and even detoxified people have come to know that these are the key places to obtain the stuff, apart from college campuses.

Interviews have revealed that the Cantonment porters are involved in selling drugs in the evenings. That is the time abusers come in search of it and buy the needed quantum to return and have a time of kicks and high.[13]

Russel Market back streets are famous for this business, said an abuser; it was awesome and thrilling to witness the modes of selling on those streets. People ranging from small children to old men are involved in this business. Opium and marijuana, semi-synthetic opium or derivatives of that family and grass are commonly marketed in this locality.

Distribution

Drug-running is a smuggling activity having many specialised areas, it is common to find persons working for several network simultaneously, even if they have their own syndicates. The distribution of drugs is done under high vigilance and supervision. Contraband is passed on from one place to the other with a new method every time. Sometimes these operators "own" the high level people and carry on their business without Government interference.

Coordinators

These are very skilled and highly intelligent traffickers. There are, a few among them who specialise in packing, for instance:

> 9 kilograms of heroin packed in candy
> Bars and cheese packs which were seized on
> 18 November 1987, en route from Mumbai to
> New York on Air India's flight· [14]

Others are experts in moving it from one place to another, then few of them in marketing areas, and others inventing new ways and means to get the stuff to the pushers or the agents. The way traffickers coordinate things, makes it difficult for the police squad to detect and seize them. A man who is in Delhi knows what is happening down here at Bangalore. Perfect coordination, cooperation, unity and secrecy are the standards of those who rule and guide. *The Illustrated Weekly of India* records how narcotic traffickers coordinate things carefully linking various places in India and outside. Indeed, it was the steady increase in the level of trafficking and smuggling of narcotics over the past few years.

Joginder Malhotra and Yudhister Kumar, who is under arrest now, had smuggled in from Pakistan – through their contacts there – 10 kgs. of high-grade heroin in the door panels of an Ambassador car. The contraband, packed into bags, was removed from one safe house to another in New Delhi as Malhotra and Kumar tried to master a new method of smuggling the heroin westwards in tins of well-known brands of pure ghee.[15] Their activities had a great lesson to teach, *viz.,* that they are one in mind and work only for a destructive cause. Mr. Jasbir Singh Sandhu, alias Jassia, is a second generation gold-runner in Punjab with links in Pakistan. He used to traffic heroin and hashish into the UK and USA, but did not as yet have his own roster of couriers. In the mid 1987, Jessie was found to have visited Pakistan, a major supply source, and was also found to be frequently flying the Delhi-Mumbai shuttle by Indian Airlines.[16]

Another case was that of Gurbux "Sam" Bhiryani, the forty-seven year old mastermind of the organisation that annually shipped, by very conservative estimates, over a ton of heroin to the USA. Earning in the process, mind-boggling amount of rupees 599 crores to rupees 800 crores per year. He did this through a high quality heroin which was from eighty to ninety per cent pure. It was said to be available for Rupees one lakh per kilo in New Delhi and its worth shot up to rupees 50 lakhs per kilo once it landed in New York. And it was the nearly ten thousand per cent profit that drew men such as Bhiryani, year after year, into this trade and motivated them to set up elaborate networks, despite the high price to be paid if caught.[17] Look at the way these men coordinated and supervised their business. It is awesome and puzzling with these highly intelligent and skilled men working in this manner it is very difficult for the NCB group to tackle them and stop their coordination. In order to do so the NCB needs ultra-coordination and complete commitment to their cause. If any self-centred motives enter, the whole plan will collapse and drug trafficking will win over the entire world with their tactics and perfect planning.

Some superb coordinators' biographies and achievements are discussed here below to indicate how much harder the Indian Narcotic Control Bureau must work in order to control this gigantic evil empire's amazing success. India is, as it were, at war once again but, unlike in the past, the enemy is not out in the battlefield. He is amongst us. The drug baron who heads vast narcotics smuggling networks spread across the continents.[18] Therefore, one has to be alert and vigilant in this battlefield in order to strike down the number one enemy of India.

The emergence of India, in recent years, as a conductor of narcotics to the International market is reflected in the statistics of seizures made at major airports. Between 1982-1986, the quantum of hashish seized rose from 190 to 751 kgs. While that of heroin increased from less than one to eighty kilograms. The growth in seizures of ganja increased from eighteen to two hundred and sixty kilograms during the same period. From 1982-1987, the pattern of drug running has been crystallising with Mumbai and Delhi as the receiving and distributing centres. Their coordination is rapidly improving day by day and bringing incredible profit to them. How then, the Narcotic Control Bureau is going to stop this menace?[19]

Here is the fascinating biographical sketch of a drug-runner who is an international coordinator and organiser. He is a man of Indian origin with International links, Dr. Gurdev Singh Sangha, initiated the Indo-Dutch connection into the heroin racket of Canada. His is the incredible story of a penniless Indian who migrated to the UK as a labourer in the late 1950s, earned an Engineering degree and then obtained a doctorate in laser technology while in Britain. Sangha then went on to set up a billion dollar narcotics network for smuggling hashish from India to Canada.

Sangha's name first attracted media attention when he, along with some Pakistanis, were arrested at Liverpool's dock in 1968 and one hundred and eighty-six kilograms of hashish were seized from them. Convicted for the offence, Sangha was incarcerated or imprisoned for three years and while he was there, he studied laser technology. After his release in 1971, he tried to live a straight life, but, despite his qualifications, he found his past was a major blot on his career as a physicist. Frustrated as a technologist, he turned again to drug-running and set up an organisation that sent drugs from India to Canada. The Organisation had the headquarters in the Hague, barely a stone's throw from the International Court of Justice.

Sangha strategically chose the Hague as the control centre of his operations because Canada had extradition treaty neither with Netherlands nor with India, and so he would be safe from the Royal Canadian Mounted Police even if his deadly cargo gets detected. During the seventies, Sangha's operations represented the single largest conduct or channel for hashish into Canada, and he not only shipped the contraband as export cargo, but also employed scores of couriers or organised bands of people to pass on reliable information and to fly out to destinations in Canada and Europe.[20] Finally, Sangha was arrested and imprisoned. Despite strict guard arrangements, he managed to escape, placing a dummy in his bed. Then he lived in India, quite openly in Delhi, until he was arrested again by the Indian Police in Delhi on 1 September 1987. Though he was engaged in an anti-social activity, yet he boldly involved himself and gained huge amounts of money, gold and silver. The consequences of all this was imprisonment and seizure of all his property.

Special wisdom is employed by people of this kind in coordination, organization and distribution of drugs. It seems as though criminals are clever than the ordinary people and trained intelligence officers.

Gurbux Bhiryani was the most intelligent coordinator and organiser among drug runners.[21] He connected everything in a perfect way, there was not leakage in all his undertakings. He included even his family members, like cousin, and brother-in-law as lieutenants. Each drug runner seems to be unique in his mode of operation and distribution of drugs.

These international figures have recruited many young men and women and trained them in coordinating drug distribution and smuggling of drugs from one place to another. These national leaders train local leaders to be area coordinators and the coordinators coordinate the local work and push the drug into the market and to the people through pushers or peddlers. Most of the coordinators in India seemed to be from a Muslim community, including pushers, in Bangalore. This is the case even on national and international levels. In Bangalore there are more than four main coordinators: two are from the north, one from Jaipur and the other from Mumbai. The other two are local people who keep shuttling from place to place. One place is in Lingarajapuram near Banaswadi, another at Jayanagar near the slum area, and two others are in the Cantonment and Fraser town areas. These people coordinate the business at Bangalore city. These coordinators are really rowdy persons, like *Dadas* or *Gundas*. They are very tough and rough in nature and in physique too. Because of this kind of coordination they are in a way successful in their drug business which has affecting all aspects of the country's life. Police statistics show a sudden spurt in illicit drug trafficking in 1986. Over two thousand eight hundred and fifty cases of heroin were handled. The largest seizure of heroin in the world of 602 kg ever was made on 9 January 1986 in a village of Talasseri, 150 kilometers from Mumbai. In August, 1986, 473 kg. was seized from a truck in Mumbai. The question is why the seizures came down by the year 1988 as over against 1983-1987. It is not because of the Narcotics Act of 1985, or the vigilance of the NCB, because in those days contraband drugs had not captured the eye of the Government and drug smugglers took shelter under the law of the land. But when the Narcotic Bureau found out that drug smuggling is affecting the country's economy, they arrested such men. NCB statistics of seizures seem high, but today, coordinators of contraband drugs are highly skilled people who can escape by some means or another. Compared to the 1980-1984 consumption of the drug, its consumption today is more rampant and this is a severe threat to Indian society. If the seizures of the drug come down, then consumption should come down, but it has increased – why? Simple answer to this question could be smugglers, coordinators and pushers have become more alert and careful in their dealings. The network of acquisition and distribution is very skilfully run.

Pushers

Pushers are the ones who sell the drug illegally and are on the streets, college campuses, college gates, school gates and so many other places like, parks, gardens, cinema theatres, also restaurants.[23] Pushers are not the coordinators, but the ones who work under them and mainly sell the drug in a smaller quantity to the addicts. There are number of pushers in Bangalore in each locality and quite a few in the Cantonment area. They come from all walks of life and age groups such as from railway porters to small boys.

Some of them are *panshopwalas*, or betel-nut, sellers, grocery shopkeepers, candy men, rickshaw men, hotel keepers, cinema gatemen, young men, old men, college students, addicts and professionals. It is one more business which fetches an enormous gain. Hence, these young and old lives are involved despite stringent punishment if caught. The street sales of drugs vary from rupees 50 crores to rupees 75 crores per year, in Mumbai alone. It has a well established network of pushers, peddlers, coordinators and retailers.[24]

One day it was a good and puzzling experience to witness the way pushers push the drug abusers. Here is a synopsis of the experience; there was a middle aged man seated quietly half-hidden from view, and leaning on the house wall as people moved about busily. A young child of nine years ran up to a young man, whispered something and came back to the seated middle-aged man. Then the child went back to the young man and after that, he left the place. The reason why this man is using this child is that he can run and hide anywhere, but the middle aged man cannot. Therefore, they make use of children. In course of time, this kind of child becomes a skilled drug smuggler, or an addict. Both are evil as far as the child's future is concerned.

Another day, in the back streets of Russel Market, a few young people were standing and chatting. As we walked along the street, we noticed people who came, joined that group, and then disappeared. Later, as we approached, one of them came up to us and asked, "how much do you need?" We acted as if we too were in need of it. We bought rupees ten worth of grass and moved on. We had to do that because of the situation. Otherwise it would have been risky and dangerous if they found out that we were only investigators, they could have harmed us, no matter what it cost them. The drug was kept under a stone slab in a dry drain and as some of them kept chatting as well as alert on all sides, someone else took it out quickly and gave away the packet to the buyer.

The interviewed student, who is a Christian and a friend of an abuser, said that as his friend was in dire need, they took a two-wheeler and reached Jayanagar slum area. There were apparently, quite a few slum dwellers who are involved in peddling, but that day they could not find the stuff because it was exhausted and pushers were not there. As they moved further, they came to a temple, out of which came a young man who said, "I have got some, but is rupees 45 and not rupees 10 and do not come here again"[25] So, they got what they wanted and returned. The world of drug abusers knows where the stuff is, and manages to get it.

There are a few vendors who indulge in this business. Addicts and abusers know them. But others do not. Betel-nut people are famous pushers because it is easy for them to hide the drug as well as sell it in the form of betel-nut and tobacco which are sold legally in public. Auto rickshaw drivers are also pushers in Bangalore, but not as many as in Mumbai and Delhi. Nonetheless, the sale of drugs is rampant.

It is true that drugs are available at nooks and corners of our major cities. As has been discussed earlier, drug availability in different places. Rumours are afloat that chocolates, ice creams, lollipops and so on are being laced with drugs to get children hooked on the stuff. The source of this rumour can be traced to a careless, negligent and unwarranted statement made by an M.P. in the Parliament without thorough and prior verification. This rumour has gained momentum, creating in the process a great deal of anxiety and panic among parents.

An experienced drug dependent has disproved this, giving more than one reason for his assertion:

Brown sugar is very bitter to the taste. No kid would ever go in for chocolates and ice cream that are repulsive to his/her taste.

Oral consumption of brown sugar does not produce the desired "trip." The stuff has got to be smoked, chased or fixed if the user is to derive any pleasurable experience.

Rather than producing dependence, oral consumption of brown sugar would only serve to cause ulcers, jaundice, liver cirrhosis, rash and other medical complications.[26]

Other drugs, like opium, can be mixed in pan, betel-nut, or dissolved in tea. However, ice cream sellers and sellers of eatables do introduce drugs to younger children in schools. When students are let free for a few minutes, as an interval, they are approached by vendors who entice them to buy drugs and even allow them to buy on credit. The urinal place is often a good secret area for such transactions. Once the young ones experience the taste and effect of the drug, they become habituated and it is very difficult to save them or get them back to normalcy.

These youngsters, male and female, hail from all walks of life, and include school and college students, office and factory employees, salesmen and medical representatives, auto rickshaw, taxi and lorry drivers, seamen, businessmen, housewives and, of course, call girls. Surprisingly, even *pujaris*, temple priests, do not seem to have been exempted from this malaise.[27] As is evident from the above, indulgence in brown sugar is not restricted to the elite urban class only. Virtually every cross-sections of society has been affected, though in the case of females, it has been observed that addicts are apt to hail from the higher socio-economic strata.[28]

Many addicts have become pushers to support their habit. It does not require hard manual labour. It is an easy job, yet profitable. John A O'Donnel says, the male junkie, i.e., heroin addict, when he is not pushing, almost invariably turns to theft and burglary to support his habit.[29] This, then explains how that pushers can become thieves. John Peter, a PUC student of a city college, stole vehicles to the value of rupees 35,000 to sustain his habit.[30] Every second student in the college seem to have had some or the other experience with drugs or its variants at least once in his college days. This is because there are pushers everywhere, actively pushing drugs and causing a loss to the nation and affecting the society.

Trafficking in drugs which has an annual global turnover of three hundred billion dollars, is run by gangs with international ramifications,[31] says the Wisdom reporter. K. V. Govind Rao. So, then the drug network is widespread and rapidly growing in our country. What should the country do to stop this? Nothing, but fight a gigantic war against Number One enemy says Sunil Dutt, M.P. and Chairman of the Congress –I Narcotics Cell.[32] If people do not fight against it today and tomorrow, they may in turn become part of this evil network of drugs through active or passive involvement. Of course, many youngsters get trapped by unscrupulous pushers and peddlers.

According to the *Times of India* report of January 15, 2016: A new study by All India Institute of Medical Sciences (AIIMS) has found that Opioids worth 7,500 Crore are consumed in Punjab annually. Of these, heroin's share is massive Rs. 6,500 Crore. This is a startling revelation that almost all the heroin that comes to Punjab is through Pakistan border, pumped in by smugglers.[33]

The First chapter is simply a description of drugs from the scientific point of view and their production and effects on the human body from the bio-chemical perspective and the second is about how those that are described in detail scientifically get into the city, market and thereby to each individual; where they are available, who makes them available. The how of it is dealt with? And the Third chapter deals with the individual: how he, as a member of society and the church is affected, socially, religiously and economically. It tells of the problems which seem not to be ours, and too far for us to get entangled with, yet we are actually right in the middle of the problem: and some of us face it personally. So then before this happens, we should give all possible support to the Narcotic Control Bureau to prevent this menace.

End Notes

1. M. J. Narendranath, "Guest Editorial," *Aikyatha*, No. 6 & 7, June-July 1987, p. 1.
2. *Ibid.*
3. Sailesh Kottary, "Busting the Bomb," *The Illustrated Weekly of India*, 23 October 1988, p. 13.
4. "opium seized," p. 3.
5. Lawton, *Christian Response*, p. 14.
6. Lobo, *Drug Addiction*, p. 16
7. Interview with the Police Commissioner, Bangalore on 25 November, 1987
8. ".... opium seized," p. 3.
9. Interview with Mr.`A', a medical student, Bangalore, on 27 November, 1987.
10. Interview with Mr. `B'. An engineering student, Bangalore, on 24 November, 1987.
11. Interview with Mr.`C' medical student, Bangalore, on 24 November, 1987.
12. Interview with Mr. `D', theological student, Bangalore, 16 November, 1987.
13. Interview with Prabhu (Pseudonym), an Engineer, Bangalore, 20 November, 1987.
14. Kottary, "The Bomb" *Weekly*, p. 10.
15. *Ibid.*, p. 13.
16. *Ibid.*, p. 10
17. *Ibid.*, p. 9
18. *Ibid.*
19. *Ibid.*, p. 12.
20. *Ibid.*, pp.14-15.
21. *Ibid.*, pp. 16-17.

22. Hire Singh, Director, National Institute of Social Defence Ministry of Welfare, Government of India, "Drug Abuse," n.d.
23. Lobo, Drug Addiction, p. 17.
24. *Indian Express* of 15 December, 1986
25. Interview with Babu (not his real name), Engineering student, Bangalore on 25 November 1987.
26. Lobo, *Drug Addiction*, p. 18.
27. *Ibid.*, p.19.
28. *Ibid.*
29. John A. O'Donnell (ed.) *Narcotics Addiction* (London: Harper and Row, 1966), p. 20.
30. "Drug Addict held for Stealing vehicles," *The Times of India*, Daily newspaper, Bangalore, 2 July, 1987.
31. K.V. Govind Rao (ed.) *Wisdom*, June 1988, p. 20.
32. Fernandes (ed.) *Care*. p. 9.
33. Shimona Kunwar, "Punjab Sinking in Pak drugs worth 7,500 crores/yr. AIIMS," *The Times of India*, Pune edition, Friday, January 15, 2016, p. 1.

Chapter 3

Socio-Religious and Economic Effects

The previous chapters discussed the drugs and their effects, also how drugs are acquired and distributed unlawfully in India. This kind of clandestine stuff affects the country's socio-religious and economic life, irrespective of caste, colour and creed. Thus, the focus of this chapter is on the lifestyle of the people in society and their struggle to cope with miseries of the world, such as the drug malady. So, the society is puzzled by the drug menace. Religion appears to have lost its moral authority over drug abusers and has nothing to say to them. The economy of an individual, family, society and the country, is being channelized into wrong uses because drug abusers have been negatively impacted by society, religion and economic status. Their take on drugs in the 1980s is as much as an expression of revolt against the ills of society, as drinking was for the young generation of the 1950s.[1] Thus, the impact and effects are on both sides, i.e., society, religion and economy play a major role in making drug addicts, and drug addicts in turn have a greater impact on all these aspects of the country's life.

Addiction is no respecter of class, sex or economic status. It is found among all races and economic levels. Young and old, alike, are affected by the tragic results of chronic usage. The addict or abuser often engages in a variety of amoral and criminal activities. The effect of the drug leaves him/her vulnerable to participate in many anti-social activities.[2] Men frequently turn to burglary to gain money needed to purchase drugs, while women often resort to prostitution.

Socio-economic environment and religio-cultural heritage impact youngsters in many ways. Students from similar social and economic backgrounds tend to draw together. Their experiences are similar, and they can easily identify with one another. These peer groups provide a setting for reinforcing common values, beliefs, attitudes and activities.[3] According to the interviewees, most of them wanted to be accepted by their peer groups, therefore they had to do what the others in the group did. This has been one of the major causes of young people getting hooked on drugs. Any other person who is not of their economic, social and cultural background will not be accepted easily. However, it is strange to note that among addicts they do not show such barriers, once they are hooked on the drug. At this stage, it does not matter who he is, as long as the other person provides some drug to satisfy his craving and accompanies him in drug-taking fellowship.

Drug addiction is the result of social and personal disorganisation because the deviant behaviour of an individual depends upon the structure of society, religion, class and economic background. Then what is a society?

> A society is a relatively independent or self-sufficient population characterised by internal organisation, territoriality, cultural distinctiveness, and sexual recruitment.[4]
>
> or
>
> A society is a group of human beings sharing a self-sufficient system of action which is capable of existing longer than the lifespan of an individual, the group being recruited at least in part by the sexual reproduction of the members.[5]

> Society is a system of human organisations generating distinctive cultural patterns and institutions and usually providing protection, security, continuity and a national identity for is members.[6]

In common terms, it could be defined as a group of people living together in a network of knit community. If this is what a society is, where an individual person plays a key role, then it is easy to assess the effects on a society when an individual portrays deviant behaviour. The individual is related to small groups which are essential part of social organisations; they are a family, peer group, work force, etc. These groups relate to an individual and an individual to a larger unity of social organisation.

Religious community and economic status come under the umbrella of a society. A society is loose term not pointing to a particular group, but used in a broader sense. It could be used for animal society, or plant society: here it means only human society, and the role of an individual for the building of society or vice versa.

Individual

An individual is a key person in any society. The humanism theory exalts an individual to the extent of being master of himself. On the other hand, communism lays emphasis on the community in which an individual loses his/her identity. But the point here is not to put man on either of these extreme levels, but to show how important a role an individual could play in developing or destroying society. Drug abuse has challenged the future life of an individual. Drugs destroy all the beautiful values of life and lead them even to murder and suicide.[7] When drug abuse becomes rampant, it is a serious threat to families, institutions and society as a whole.

An individual's youth can be one of the happiest stages of his life. The changing standards of the world and its problems have robbed youth of their happiness. Drug addiction among college students, especially professional students, is the result of a multiplicity of factors, like disintegration of social structures, rapid and unplanned industrialisation, urbanisation and cultural and socio-economic crises have aggravated the problem. An individual is under pressure of choosing the best of life and the peer group's recognition and identity of his/her peer society and the pleasure of his own self.

The individual here is mainly a reference to the student; also occasional reference is made to every age group. A drug addict is an individual person but he causes several kinds of social evils. "There is a rough estimate that fifteen thousand young drug addicts are being added to our nation every year."[8] A recent interview at Bangalore revealed that nearly eighty-five per cent of medical and engineering students in one or the other use drugs. Hence, the statement, "the youth of a nation are the trustees of prosperity," is under a question mark because of the increase in drug abuse among college students.

Today, students who are hooked on drugs are led into crimes and prostitution to sustain their habits. John Peter, a PUC student of a city college, stole rupees 35,000 worth vehicles from the Cantonment areas of Bangalore, Frazer town, Lingrajapuram and Wilson Garden area. This is illustrated here to show social evil though it is mentioned elsewhere. *Blitz* of 22 August, 1987 records that four young girls sold their bodies to obtain drugs, and they became streetwalkers/prostitutes.[9] These individual addicts have caused society to bear and to experience new diseases, like STD, i.e., sexually transmitted disease. *The Indian Express* of 28 May, 1986 records 3,88,465 people attacked by STD in Maharashtra state alone. Tamilnadu had 1,79,534 and Karnataka 63,595 people in late 1980s.[10]

Another deadly disease is AIDS (Acquired Immune Deficiency Syndrome), mainly caused by drug addicts because most of these indulge in homosexuality and prostitution, and some drugs are specially meant to enhance the sexual feelings: when that occurs unhealthy relationships with one another does take place. In 1987, it was predicted by news agencies and doctors that there will be 180,000 deaths due to AIDS with an additional 150,000 in a critical condition within the next four years.[11] And for the information sake, there were about ten to twenty million AIDS-affected people in the

USA in 1987. In the early stage, AIDS is presently called GRID-Gay related immune deficiency. Now AIDS is spread over one hundred and fifty countries and is spreading all over the world. *Youth Care magazine* records that five people die daily in Mumbai alone due to drug consumption.[12] The video cassette produced by St Paul's Communications, Mumbai, displays the trauma of the addict and their social status. Many of these are brought to Mumbai and sold, and others have come in search of jobs and hooked by this junk. When an interviewer asked, "why did you start drug taking?" the reply was "there was nothing else to go for." Others said classmates had introduced drugs. Some were hooked because of the influence of peer groups during their teens.

Karsan, twenty-eight years of age, was a criminal gang leader who earned rupees 3000 per day by pick-pocketing, but to dull the pain of police beatings he turned to brown sugar and he ended up in jail and acquired tuberculosis during his addiction. Siraj Ahmed, a young man of twenty-seven was a petty thief. He became a peddler with five police cases against him,[13] This is a frightening situation and make us wonder what is happening and where we are heading.

Addicts steal on an average more than 6,30,00,000 property in New York every day.[14] The above mentioned illustrations and incidents are the manifestations of drug abuse. Society endures violent assault, rape, murder, new diseases, increase of streetwalkers and prostitutes, criminals and smugglers. In short, anti-social persons have caused damage to society and to themselves.

Due to these pressures that addicts have brought upon the society, they (the addicts) are considered criminals, outcastes and rejected by the society. The awkward behaviour of addicts has captured the attentions of tender-aged students, and they are made members of the world of drugs. Society looks on it as this menace is spreading evil and avoids any contact with the addicts, but has not made any effort to prevent drug-abuse. An addict said, in an interview, that society must accept us and not consider that we are rotten goods. Such a person, once he becomes an addict, is not considered as a person and not included in any major or minor decision-making in the family or in the community.

An individual's social background plays an important role in his behaviour and action. Breakdown in the family, strained relationships, lack of understanding and love, social upbringing, poverty and meaninglessness in life, make a person feel it is worthless to live and when a person goes through these crimes, he seeks to find other means whereby he could get rid of these problems and pressures. The effects of society on individuals make people go mad. Sometimes inequality, injustice, lack of concern and care for the suffering, tends to make the younger generation adopt the philosophy of 'eat, drink and be merry.' They see nothing but hopelessness, meaninglessness in their future, but what seems good is to do it today, tomorrow does not matter, and is the attitude that has crept into the minds of the new generation.

Upper class students want to experiment, enjoy the peer group and think too much of competing with the intelligence of the west and its pattern. Most of the time they want to imitate and cope with modern technology. Drugs are not the answer for all of these problems.

The way out, for modern man/woman, is to learn to live well, not apart from the strain but in it.[15]

What we require is not a formula for peace which humanly speaking is impossible, but rather "a formula for living wisely and well in the midst of continuous strain."[16] Unfortunately, it is not infused into the minds of young lives. They think they can manage their lives but they miss out by messing it up. Thus, the individual is affected in many ways, especially by the disorganised society. Now, the society is threatened by the behaviour of an addicted individual. Why do youngsters act the way they do? It is because of the influence of society on them and the attraction of modernity. Instead of meeting the moral and ethical demands of society to create a new and model environment and also instead of providing protection, security and continuity and national identity to its members, they are causing chaos and confusion with their drug culture.

As we evaluate religious groups or communities, we find they seem to be unaware of the drug menace, and severity of its consequences. Religion is a part of society because the particular group is an essential aspect of the social organisation. Religion must not think it is mundane to get involved in social work such as creating an awareness of the drug menace and teaching the community about God. Religion has failed to give proper guidance to youngsters and to engage them in the various activities of religion. The rigid demands of religion have made youngsters think it is meaningless to invest time in its monotonous, routine activities. On the other hand, youngsters are considered too immature to participate in the religious activities of that particular group, this has led them to find more creative activities like experimenting with destructive things in life. That has been one of the reasons for youngsters to take drugs: the activities of the religion have been too impersonal. An addict said: "God does not respect us and hear us if we pray because he always listens to good people."[17] Who can remove this wrong concept from their mind? Isn't religion responsible for inculcating faith values in youngsters?

If an individual becomes an addict, probably Hinduism will consider it to be his/her *karma*, or punishment for his past evil deeds. Therefore, he is suffering now. Islam may say, Allah has predestined him/her to be so. Christianity regards him/her as a sinner who has hope in Christ. This kind of attitude turns the youngster away from religious life and practice. An individual is part and parcel of the community and the religion either he can propagate the morality and ethics of his/her religion or demoralize and corrupt or repudiate by becoming an addict. The Police Commissioner of Bangalore city said that Christian students who are studying in convent schools abuse drugs more than any other students in the Cantonment area. One may wonder, why this remark? Maybe the school has failed to discipline them or give them proper guidance and meaning in life. Poor quality of leaders and people living around would have led them to go in for this kind of fun of drug abuse.

Religious groups of any community must think and evaluate their influences on this modern generation. Addicts have "no religion,"[18] said the de-addicted person in an interview. What then is the core purpose of religion? It is to shape moral and ethical values above all spiritual attitudes and lifestyle of the person for the sake of better society. Otherwise, it may also become one more agent to produce people who are anti-socials. For them, religion has failed to affect their personality; as a result, they are affecting the religious life of the society by engaging in evil and immoral activities and following unethical standards influencing the growing children of our nation, in a given community.

Each individual is responsible for the economy of the country, society, the family and even personal economy. But, drugs which have no positive effect on human life are consuming millions of rupees. Smugglers and coordinators operate in crores and lakhs. How is that? Where does the money come from? This kind of operation definitely affects the country.

The purpose here is not to show the country's defects but of an individual. Most of the students who spend on drugs come from well-off families. The re-recovered addict gave a testimony over the radio on 10 November, 1980 to the fact that he is able to spend money lavishly as his parents do not ask for an account. Later, he started taking things from the house, finally, he was cast out of the family then he went to Mumbai, became worse by indulging in all kinds of dirty work to sustain his habit.[19] Another addict said on video that he had a joint account with his father and spent money as he liked. Finally, he got caught and was taken to hospital for treatment.[20] One other student said he had started stealing small things at home and his mother was lenient with him. She did not disclose his behaviour to his father. Later, he was found to be an addict and they took him for treatment. However, who can help these friends who come from the lower strata of the society? (An addict said, looking at the other addicts).

Money is channelled into wrong uses. Wealth and health are both lost, nothing is gained but a momentary pleasure and excitement.

Due to heavy dependence on drugs, an individual gets involved in crime, burglary, cheating, peddling drugs, stealing and so many other anti-social activities. Women turn to prostitution, selling their bodies for the drugs, and they have become the street walkers mentioned earlier. For them to be rehabilitated or restored back to normalcy is very difficult. An addict in an interview said once I went to a hospital and requested them to help me out of this problem, but they saw me and sent me back empty-handed.[21] Many slum dwellers are hooked by this drug. They are not in a position to come out of it because of their economic conditions.

An employee who is an addict becomes inefficient in his work performance; hence his services gets terminated. The only way out for him is to go in for stealing in order to sustain his habit. The consequence is, his dependants suffer and are made beggars. Students lose interest in their studies, sell their belongings to obtain drugs and most of them borrow and become debtors. In most cases, they cannot repay, since they do not have any financial resources.

So, then the socio-religious and economic effects on the individuals are heavy. In the end, both suffer, - the individual and the society, due to drug abuse and addiction. Society's hope in the individual becomes in vain, and the individual loses his confidence in his society, but builds self-confidence by taking drugs. Social, religious and economic effects shape an individual's personality. Therefore, all the three aspects are being challenged to re-evaluate their functions for the welfare of humanity and the purpose of their existence on this planet earth.

Family

The family is a foundational and fundamental unit in any given society. A family could be called a cell, in a larger society. It has a greater role to give a right perspective to society. It has a greater role to give a right perspective to society. Family government, economy and religion depend on the kind of persons the family has. Once there is a breakdown, it not only affects the family and its members, but the whole of society. It is like a small fire catching the whole forest. A family is not in an isolation to be able to act independently. Its failure as well as its success will inevitably have an impact on society. A breakdown of the family may not be the concern of the neighbour and society, but it will have its repercussion on society in due time.

William Enright said one of the greatest concerns of today is the collapse of the family as a meaningful unit in the society ... yet homes are too often split-level traps from which youngsters want to flee. So, often each member of a family goes his or her separate way. Consequently, family relations are fractured or frozen at best, the members do not know each other, and what is worse, many do not care.[22] Therefore, what is important in the family relationship is love and accepting one's fault with humility and teachability. "Happy families are all alike; every unhappy family is unhappy in its own way,"[23] said Leo Tolstoy.

Successful family living is in many ways rather like playing a game in unity and integrity. Each member of the ensemble has his own skills, his own special knack with the part he chooses to play, but the grace and strength and sweetness of the performance comes from everyone's willingness to subordinate individual virtuosity and personal ambition to the requirements of balance and blend. Children learn first and best from their families, so their behaviour is stamped with the seal of their adult protectors. The family unit is often cited as the single, most powerful influence on a child's life. The amount of teaching, modelling, correction, and influence that can only occur within the family environment far surpasses the input from other sources and greatly influences the adolescent's adaption to his or her world.[24] The family was never intended to be structureless and disordered. Indeed there is nothing more disruptive of the family than the absence of structure and order.[25] The lack of these will have repercussions on the larger family, i.e., society. If the family is in order, it will reflect on the society as families are the social units or cells which together constitute the human community. Disorder in the family gives rise to disastrous disharmony in society at the very point where there should be the most perfect accord (the family).[26]

The members of the family both parents and children, each one is important individual in the whole structure. Parents who consistently express love and affection and provide meaningful discipline and explain consequence for misbehaviour, establish an optimal healthy family environment for their children.[27] "Children are the greatest joy and social security, in a sense they are **insurance for old age.**"[28] They are also the active agents in stimulating family friendship and neighbourly contacts. But what is happening in most of the families in India today is that sad picture altogether, what has been discussed so far is the model family which is expected by the society. On the other hand most of the city families are in shambles, because there is a generation gap, parents are not able to understand their children and children do not understand the traditional value setup and upbringing of the parents. Today's youngsters want freedom and to live in a carefree lifestyle and enjoy life in the way they think is right. As a result they indulge in unhealthy activities like drug abuse and addiction. What could be the reasons for the way they act today?

Possible Reasons

1. Perfectionist parents continually demand perfection from their children who feel that they can never be good enough. Consequently, they have feelings of inadequacy, discouragement and deep self hate which leads to depression and hostility towards their parents. This situation at home causes them to take shelter under peer groups and they learn to identify with these groups in all aspects.
2. Unloving parents and rejection leads them to find acceptance and warmth with people outside the family.
3. Authoritative parents – dictatorial parenthood is not appreciated, though it might work up to a certain phase in children's life and what happens after certain age is there for everyone to see. Children rebel to numerous pressures and they feel helpless and alienated.[29]
4. Uncontrolled freedom – leads youngsters to choose anything that seems best at that moment in time.

5. Lack of healthy and transparent communication within the family members.
6. Breakdown and strained relationships among the family members or among the parents which has an indirect impact on the growing children.
7. Lack of educative information to the children from the parents and the elders in the family.
8. The lifestyle of parents. There are parents who do not have time for their children; they are under the care of baby sitters/nannies. They probably think giving children plenty of money is a substitute for their love and care.
9. Lack of inculcating fear of God, faith values and moral standards in its family members.
10. Poverty and inability to cope with society.
11. Superficial relationships in the family and not being open to one another, individualistic behaviours – living for oneself. Not being concerned about other family members welfare and forgiving and seeking forgiveness from each another etc.
12. Rigidity and traditionalism in family which creates a huge gap between the young and the old thereby leading each member to go their own ways without respecting the other.
13. Lack of confidence and trust among the family members. Suspecting children all the time may lead to breakdown of mutual trust, could lead to alienation, prompting them to seek acceptance elsewhere.

Most of the interviewees revealed that as children they were not treated properly, their struggles were not understood, so they became frustrated and dejected, due to the family setup. Some who were of the upper strata of the society were not directed properly, but let free on their own. Parents had no time to listen to their children to understand their problems and help and guide them in times of need.[30] There was a great relational vacuum created and, in the course of time, it was filled with the wrong ideology, i.e., eat, drink and be merry: and finally, end up with peer groups and drugs; all because their hunger for understanding, acceptance and recognition remained unfulfilled and dissatisfied in life. The alternative to cope with this situation was to go for drugs. This seems to be a ground reality in many homes today.

Having experienced the kind of a family, they feel it is senseless to live, an inability to turn to others for comfort, inability to articulate and involve themselves in meaningful, purposeful and constructive activity. They experience feelings of hurt, rage, shame, loneliness, aggression and depression, negative self-concept, sense of profound failure, weakness, guilt, self-doubt, confusion and despair, while going through these crises they resort to drugs which enable them to forget their troubles and be in their own world. Among the addicts some are extroverts who abuse stimulants and are resistant to conditioning for social values and hence tend to show an anti-social propensity. Introverts are pre-disposed to abuse depressant drugs.[31]

Drug-addicted children will become rebellious to the religious and social norms at home and outside, aggressive and dominant, wanting to gain control over their environment and over others at home. Suppressed feelings result in angry actions which are turned against society and others around them. Religion and economy are not heeded and thus, the family economy drains and religion becomes a meaningless practice. Many families wail and mourn because they see their children's lives ruined by drug addiction. The productive and happy future they have foreseen for their children has turned to despair and hope turned to heartbreak.[32] Parents are amazed and are lost at the staggering drug menace and its power to ruin prospective future leaders.

It is advisable and better for the families to communicate their faith and convictions at an early stage and solve their initial problems with love. To do this one may need a structured programme for approaching such a situation:

1. Do not panic – but evaluate the situation and the condition. Instead of doing this, some parents manhandle the child, some take the situation lightly, and others feel guilty of failure to protect their child. What the child needs is wise counselling and careful undoing of the present condition.

2. Learn to communicate – heart-to-heart and eyeball-to-eyeball contact, in other words, straight communication helps to understand his/her misery/behaviour.
3. Evaluate the problem – how severe it is, and whom to contact in such situation.
4. Follow through – they need strict supervision, observation and involve them in all family affairs. Let them know that they are important and are cared for.
5. Try hard to prevent carefully and cautiously the problem as you spot it.[33]

An individual gets affected because of the drug abuse; socially, religiously and economically. This affects the family severely, not one suffers, but the whole family suffers with an addict. If an individual and the family are affected, and they do not do anything about it, the whole community or neighbourhood and society becomes the victim in one way or the other. One student becoming an addict in the family causes tension and disturbance in the normal life of the society. An individual is an important pillar of the society. If the family falls, it is a definite sign that society will also decline in terms of its religious, moral and economic life.

Neighbourhood

A neighbour is a person who lives next door and nearby to another fellow being, or those who live around him/her: by neighbouring, in this context meant a community or a small group which strengthens the person's social bonds and conditions, his moral character and value system. This community supplies the basis for social solidarity and group cohesion in larger scale organisations. It is a common understanding that a, 'man is a social animal'. He/she likes to move freely in society, build one's relationships and friendships, wants to love and be loved. But the awkward or indifferent behaviour of a person blocks the door of the neighbours for such friendly relationships. It all depends on an individual's personality trait, whether he is accepted or rejected by a community. People in general would prefer to live in harmony and in cooperation with their neighbours. The moment they observe that the neighbour's son is a spoilt child, they can never think of allowing their children to move with them and even cut off their relationships from that family. Ostracism is a great blow to anybody in society. They become suspicious about the student next door. It has been said, "If you want to know what someone is like, look at his friends."[34] Our association with kind of people will reflect one's values, beliefs and attitudes.

Once the youngster or college student is spotted as being a drug abuser, neighbours will think twice before allowing their children to accompany him to school or college. Socialising is curtailed and most of the hooked people start everything under the shadow and in darkness. They lose their social and religious values and are suspected by the neighbours every time, that is why the statement saying our characters or lifestyles either block the doors or break the barriers. In the case of an addict, the door gets blocked. If one has an unpleasant neighbour, the odds are that he too is one, said Frank A. Clark.[35] When this happens in the community, the whole community is under mockery, black marked. To remove the mark one has to cultivate and develop personality. The social laboratory of living and learning with brothers and sisters teaches a young person many beliefs about the self and others that will be carried through life.[36]

Neighbours are awakened to the fact that drug abuse is a social evil that has to be prevented. One of the drawbacks in the cities is the nuclear family system which hardly gives any chance for children to grow in a company of their age group. When they are exposed in schools and colleges they choose their own peer group and join in all sorts of habits. A reserved personality could be one of the results of this nuclear family system.

Drug abuse has prevented neighbours from letting their children move freely and learn social values. Their religion is under mockery and the economic condition affects the whole community. Things are missing in the neighbours' house, and they are troubled and disturbed by the addicts around them. The police commissioner's statement repeated here that "Christian students in the Cantonment area are the biggest drug abusers."[37] What an insulting remark to the whole community, as well as to the locality. Handful youngsters involved in drug addiction bringing shame and disrespect to the whole area due to their bad habits is unfortunate. Thus, impersonal relationships, non-cooperation, non-supportive attitudes will be obvious. Individual, family and neighbours are linked together; they all need one another to live and to work. One cannot be independent for a long period, one need other persons: encouragement, support and help; so if one has gone astray the whole community suffers in socio-religio-economic spheres.

The community or neighbourhood that is discussed here is not a particular community or faith, but it is used in a general sense, referring to all faiths and cultures with which one comes in contact in day-to-day life.

Since all communities or neighbourhoods are greatly affected by drug addiction, some suggestive measures for the local community to control the drug menace will not be out of place, even when applied to the broader level.

1. Seek ways to control the abuse of all addictive substances within your setting.
2. Educate your members about the seriousness of substance abuse within the family and social system.
3. Integrate local religious programmes to educate, prevent, treat, rehabilitate and to give after-care,
4. Provide continuous reassurance about your own interest and involvement in the welfare of the addict and his/her family.
5. Help the addict and his/her family with the available medical, social and legal assistance to the problems which may have arisen as a result of drug abuse.
6. Continue your supportive visit to the families of the addicts and develop new and innovative resources for the help of the addicts and their families.[38]
7. Take the drug abuse seriously as it concerns the whole community and exhibit dreadful consequences of drug use, misuse and abuse. The communities can play a major role

in preventive programmes; they boost the work of NCB of India, since our neighbourhood is the most affected area of the nation.

Church

The church is a chosen community of God, entrusted with a specific task to perform on earth under the headship of the triune God. When problems challenge society, the church is not excluded, it is very much a part of them. It has homework to do and concern to show. Drug abuse is not away from the Church; it is in fact entering subtly and capturing the minds of the youth, and students in particular. Hence, the church cannot have a "holier than thou" attitude.[39] and behave like Ostrich in times of danger burying its head into the sand; toward an affected country or society. Jesus said: "you are in the world but not of the world," so then, when anything happens to the world, the Church is definitely affected and must be concerned about all aspects that concern its welfare.

Socio-religious and economic effects are already noticed in the church. The interviewed pastors of different parishes in Bangalore seem to be unaware of the drug problem. Some of them know, but have not taken any action because most of them are busy in administration, evangelisation among non-Christians, conferences, committees and preaching sermons on Sundays, also on weekdays. Therefore, they find no time for this issue. Some have dealt with drug addicts but most of them conceal their children' drug problems. Therefore, pastors have not found it a big problem. But articles in journals, magazines, newspapers and unpublished papers exhibit the severity of the problem among the younger generation, most of whom are college students.

The church will lose youngsters coming for worship services. Future church leadership will be hindered because bright young students are under the gigantic evil empire. Socially the addicts' parents would prefer to withdraw from spiritual activities in order to retain their social prestige. As a result, the church becomes thinner day by day, and so, the church has to get on to the battlefield to fight against this evil. If the true religion such as Christianity is not for saving a soul, then why should it exist? The command of Jesus Christ to the church is to be a light, and salt, on the earth; not just one of the sects or groups, or communities. The church has to be sensitive to the increasing evil of drug abuse. Detaching, detecting, evaluating and delivering the human life which is in the bondage of drugs is the moral obligation of the church. It cannot afford to lose its potential future leaders and ministers. A man who was a member of the criminal mafia group was saved, and he now works as an evangelist among the addicts in Switzerland.[40] a great turning point in Billy Graham's convention.

The Church is to follow the Master's footsteps to lose its life for the cause of saving one. "The truth is that we gain a sense of importance for our lives by losing them and we lose them by devoting them to some ideal, particularly an ideal embodied in a concrete cause."[41] For this, the Church has to recognise the danger that has come into society, and teach emphatically to resist the detected problem, namely drug abuse, with the power of God and His weapons. **A Church that is not reaching out is passing out** said Duke Basson.[42] Thus the Church must exercise its spiritual authority by taking up social responsibility in the world. The Church is the shepherding agent in the world, inviting everyone to faith in Christ. Hence, Charles C. Morrison said: *The Christian Church is the only society in the world in which membership is based upon the qualifications that the candidate shall be unworthy of membership.*[43]

The Church's responsibility for other persons is that of exhortation of the peril, becoming one's keeper and bearing one another's burden. Otherwise, the Church will be held responsible on **that day** for the eternal death of an individual who died in sin knowing that he was living in sin. The Church not only serves humanity on the spiritual level, but it has the responsibility for the whole person. Basic physical and social needs are to be met because human being is both physical and social creature, as well as a spiritual being.[44]

Of course, the social responsibility of the Church is first to its own, to the self and family. The Scriptures exhort, **Do good to all men**, without any discretion between the poor and the rich, educated and illiterate, masters and slaves, elite and oppressed. All that is required of the Church is to promote peace, morality and Christ in this world. Togetherness of the community and its edification are the testimony of the Church. The Church is well defined in I Corinthians 12, Romans 12 and in the Epistles to the Galatians. It is reconciled, but the addict is in error, nearer to death, without hope, groping in darkness, restless and at enmity with God. So, the purpose of God in the world is evident in the nature of the Church to reconcile persons to Himself and to restore their lives to natural order.[45]

The Church indeed suffers because society suffers, of which it is a part. Religion has failed to influence its members to lead a moral and ethical life. Drug abuse is no respecter of caste and class: religion and society: but affects every institution and individual. The church's spiritual authority and its existence will be questioned; its evangelising programme will become mockery. Because, if the church has a problem with its own members, where does the effect of evangelism be seen? Therefore, drug abuse is not only a social evil; it is both an economic and a religious evil. All these aspects suffer as a result of drug abuse. Since it is a major disturbing and threatening menace, one should fight against it.

End Notes

1. Interview with Marcia Michael, OMS Secretary, SAIACS Bangalore on 7 December, 1987.
2. Clyde M. Narramore, *Encyclopedia of Psychological Problems* (Grand Rapids: Zondervan Publishing House, 1981), p. 123.
3. G. Keith Olson, *Why Teenagers Act the Way They Do* (Loveland: Group Books, 1987), p. 57.
4. *International Encyclopaedia of the Social Sciences*, s.v. "Society."
5. *Ibid.*
6. *Collins Dictionary of the English Language*, s.v. "Society."
7. N. F. Fernandes (ed.) "The Time to Act is Now," *Indian Youth Care*, Vol. I, No. 3, November 1986, p. 9.

8. Fr. Stanley Coelho, "Drug Addiction and Counselling for Change," a paper presented at Vellore Counselling Centre, n.d.
9. "Give me little Gard," *Blitz.* 22 August, 1987, pp. 11, 19.
10. *Indian Express*, daily newspaper, 28 May, 1986.
11. "Aids : A Scientific and Christian Perspective," *Light of Light*, April 1988.
12. Fernandes, (ed.) "The Time to Act ...." *Youth Care,* p. 9.
13. "Gard Ka Rasta," postscript, *The Indian Post,* Sunday, 5 July, 1987.
14. Richard D' Souza, "Drugs Key to Seal Living" *Youth Care,* Vol. I, No. 1, July - August 1986, p. 6.
15. Elton Trueblood, *The Life We Prize* (WACO: A World Books, 1972), p. 42.
16. Ibid.
17. "Is anybody listening?" (Video tape film) Bombay: St Paul's Communication, Daughters of St Paul, Interviews and Testimonies, 1987.
18. Interview with Ramu, a student of City College, Bangalore, 5 December, 1987.
19. Testimony, broadcast from Radio Station, Bangalore on Thursday, 10 November, 1987.
20. Video tape testimony, produced by the Daughters of St. Paul, Bombay 1987.
21. *Ibid.*
22. Llyod Cory, *Quotable Quotations* (Wheaton: Victor Books, 1983), p. 132.
23. *Ibid.*
24. Olson, *Why Teenagers Act*, p. 32.
25. Philip E. Hughes, *Christian Ethics in Secular Society* (Grand Rapids: Baker Book House, 1984), p. 153.
26. *Ibid.*, p. 154.
27. Olson, *Why Teenagers Act*, p. 33
28. Gerhard Lohfind, *Jesus and the Community* (London: SPCK, 1985), p. 41.
29. Olson, *Why Teenagers Act*, pp. 33f.
30. Cory, *Quotations*, p. 272.
31. Abraham Verghese, "Drug Abuse among the Adolescent," Professor and Head of the Department of Psychiatry, CMC, Vellore, 1987.
32. M. C. B. J. Raja, "Towards a drug free society," *Aikyata* No. 4, April 1987, p. 1.
33. Donald B Louria, *Overcoming the Drugs* (New York: McGraw Hill Book Company, 1971), pp. 116f.
34. Olson, *Why Teenagers Act*, p. 45.
35. Cory, *Quotations*, p.162.
36. Olson, *Why Teenagers Act*, p. 46.
37. Interview with Police Commissioner, Special Squad, Bangalore, 15 November 1987.
38. Bass Babu (ed.), "Addiction: Church's Responsibility," *South India Churchman*, August 1987.

39. Milton L Rudnick, *Christian Ethics for Today* (Grand Rapids: Baker Book House, 1979), p. 115.
40. Interview with Suri Williams, Area Director of YFC, Sri Lanka, Bangalore, 5 July 1987.
41. Trueblood, *Life We Prize*, p. 51.
42. Cory, *Quotations*, p. 68.
43. *Ibid.*, p. 67.
44. Normal L Geisler, *Ethics* (Grand Rapids: Academic Books, Zondervan, 1971), p. 180.
45. Joe S Ellis, *The Church on Purpose* (Cincinnati: Standard Publishing, 1982), p. 33.

Chapter 4

Biblical and Ethical Perspectives of Drug Abuse

In the first three Chapters, the discussion has been concentrated on the inflow and effect of drugs on human life. This grave societal ill troubles everyone. Is there any redemptive answer or hope for those affected? Of course there may be several theoretical suggestions without hope, or there may be several philosophical programmes which may not reach troubled human beings or different religious groups may promote penance, pilgrimage, fasting and prayer, as a solution to this staggering menace in India. Many of these philosophical, theoretical and superb ideas are appreciated; the mere principles and philosophies may not be relevant for they do not solve the problems of the present context crises effectively.

Can one talk with splendid eloquence and authority on philosophy and the theory of life and its ethics? Will it become a source of reformation, restoration and rehabilitation for addicts? Is there anyone listening to their cry, and meeting the deep needs of their mind and heart? What are the people searching for through drugs in their lives? Well! These are good questions, to ponder and resolve to act decisively against this menace. Today, drug abuse is mentioned almost every day in major newspapers of India. Magazines give details of seized cases. Few Christians have published books written by Yusuf A Merchant entitled, *Brown Sugar Addiction*; Benjamin Lobo, *The Answer to Drug Addiction*: And Michael O'Toole, *Drugs and Youth in India,* etc.

Committees and conferences are held to discuss problems of drug abuse and this is a much debated topic, but the result is a numerical increase of about fifteen thousand drug addicts every year in our country. To aggravate further, the production of illicit drugs and the import of contraband is on the increase. What then is the solution, and where does the problem lie? Can it be solved?

There must be a solution to this problem. All the talk, discussion, conferences and publications, Government and private sector efforts to prevent drug abuse is like *chopping of the branches while allowing the tree to grow*. Trying to eliminate the effects, not the effecting factors have been the cause for widespread increase. It is like being bewildered at the burning fire, and not making any efforts to quench it. When we get down to grass root level to analyse and understand the root cause of the problem, one recognises that it is not that easy to fight against the enemy without a proper understanding of the problem and employing the right strategies.

Human effort may fail but divine power is the ultimate answer for our societal predicaments. God can only recreate, reform and restore human's distorted personality. Man/woman is essentially a sinner, his/her fallen nature resorts to anything that seems better for the moment and seeks to gratify the flesh. Therefore, this chapter seeks to discuss what man/woman is, his/her nature, purpose and destiny in life. Conditioning the ethical and moral demands on him/her with Biblical and ethical perspectives and trying to answer the queries raised in the earlier chapter.

Biblical Perspective

Drugs are being used to avoid the problems of life, and reality. It is an escape route of living in a dream world. How long will it last? May be for a couple of days or months, or even years, then what next?

One cannot escape the reality of life. One has to learn to live with it, though it is not easy. However, the Christ of faith and the Jesus of history gives practical guidelines through His inspired word and not with a philosophical eloquent speech. Human being wants to try many things to find peace and joy and a sense of wellbeing. Drugs are not the answer for the problems of life when truth is realised in the heart about life, there comes a revealed purpose and meaning of existence on this globe.

The use and abuse of drugs is not in conformity to God's standards and character. It enslaves man and woman and denies God's purpose for them. Addiction deprives them of abundant living and true happiness and is a denial of God's fullness of life. Abusers do not understand the preciousness and worth of living, but see it as mere excitement and fun. They are playing with life which they think is not their own. One must know that we are destined to live the remainder of our lives in tension and turmoil. Whatever lies ahead, it is not a course of tranquillity instead of pining for calmer days, the way of wisdom is to live realistically in such a time of stress and strain.[1] Instead of facing the stress and strain, people run for drugs. In the end, they destroy their own lives and influence the whole of humanity to indulge in wrong practices. They come under bondage of addiction, controlled by drugs, and thus, heading towards destruction. Drug abuse is against God, against law, society, religion and one's own self. Yet they go for them – why? They have not understood the reality of life and misuse the freedom that has been given to them.

Manifestations of drug addiction and its abuse are vehemently condemned in the Bible - the Word of God; but not the addict or the abuser. God's word gives this wonderful hope even while we are living in sin and rejecting the loving and caring invitation of God, and the quickening work of the Holy Spirit. Addicts are not able to see beyond momentary excitement, their eyes are blinded to the truth, and to the future. Self-fulfilment is their philosophy for the day. OS Guiness, in *Dust of Death* says that drugs are "totally unnecessary either as a way to gain meaning or an escape ... they are unhelpful."[2] In the context of Biblical truth, the Bible nowhere permits persons to use their body as one pleases, since he/she has no authority over his/her own life. The experience of drugs is an illusion, unreal, momentary and harmful to oneself and to society as a whole. Non-abusers in the society are not those who have no problems, but those who have determined to live under continued and increasing strain. This kind of life is essentially the same for all but the reactions of different persons to it differ radically. Some continue with this life and hope for the better, while others try to escape by means of drugs. This result in destruction and death which are rewards that comes before their time.

Therefore, we must concentrate on the theology of man/woman and his ethics to gain a correct perspective to the whole framework of man. Attempts will be made to clarify some of the misconceptions of a humanistic philosophy of human being and the misunderstanding of meaningful living, among youngsters who indulge in drug abuse. The Bible is the only Divine Book that gives a clear picture of human person and the duties he/she has to fulfil. It may appear while reading the Bible, from the beginning to the end, that it only talks about human beings, his/her activities and duties. But he/she is acting under the direction of God who is invisible. Human being is majestic and reflects the wonder of the Creator whose image they bear.[3] This chapter will explore the various dimensions of human person to reaffirm the Biblical dignity of man and woman in an age of dreadful assault upon humanity. Scripture affirms that man is the crown of Creation and has dual purposes to perform: one is to God, and the other to the nature or creation, because he/she has been created in the image of God.

Man and Woman are Created in the Image of God

Life did not spring out of nature by some evolutionary process. Human being is the result of the immediate action of God. On the other hand, he/she is not divine but mortal, and has to live with struggles, difficulties, diseases, and the uncertainty of human's life journey. However, unconditionally, we cannot annihilate human, nor evacuate, evaporate or extenuate them. For human is not only a contributory creature, but a total creature; he/she does not only make one, but he/she is all. He/she is not a piece of the world but the world itself, and next to the Glory of God, the reason why there is a world, said John Donne in his sermon on 8 May 1625.[4] It gives a profound climax to the creation process. Hence, human being stands before God in a relationship of created dependence and also has the status of unique and special personhood in relation to God.

Human being shares with nature and the activities of nature shares with them. Nature is made to serve them and they are to tend it. Nature is not a neutral entity in relation to human beings.[5] They are to reflect the nature and love of God in their activities, lifestyle and their whole being. They cannot act on their own with regard to their heart and soul for they can cause their beings to deteriorate gradually by the unnatural intake of unhealthy chemicals like drugs.

Human being is not pictured in the Bible as materialistic scientists present them. In their view, man appeared by chance or came into being: he has no hope, no value, but is just an entity. To them, a man is of no importance: instead a machine has become "more human" than man.[6] However, human beings possess a dignity that far surpasses that of a machine, animal and technology. It is to God human is drawn, not anything else: they talk with God and are very distinct from the other creations of God in many ways. *Only human being has the breath of God that no other creature has.* Therefore, they are unique in many ways. Human being is created, he/she is not the creator, human is dependent, not independent. He/she is akin to the great elephant as well as to the lizard and the sparrows. Like them human is dependent upon a complex spectrum of factors for their existence. However, human is near to God than any of God's creatures. His/her differentia is that which makes them what they are, that is, they are made in the divine image of God. "Alongside the statement of human's ephemeral and limited nature the Old Testament proclaims unceasingly the eminent dignity conferred upon human beings for their peculiar associations with God."[7] Human in the image of God is a majestic and superb creature; he/she has great dignity in the eyes of their maker. Since their creation is by a totally different method.

The world was created out of nothing (Gen 2:7) and man was made from the dust of the ground and the woman from the rib of man. In both cases, God used pre-existing substance in His wonderful formation. The essential issue is that man was created by an act of God. When God made man He made something entirely new in the created order. Dietrich Bonhoeffer said:

> Man shall proceed from God as His ultimate, His new work, and as the image of God in His creation. There is no transition here from somewhere or other, there is new creation.[8]

This high conception of man is a wonder if not anti-religious: it is a pure revealed theology. Human being is God's greatest handiwork, fashioned in the divine image. It is in the image of God that man has his dignity. This stand should not be misunderstood that man is created in the image of God, and therefore, is a little less than God. This thought makes him a kind of superman, who lives in the air. No, not true. We must keep in mind that man was made from the dust of the ground; this demonstrates his continuity with the physical world. Though man is nearer and has a unique relationship with God, yet he continues to live with other creatures. The image of God in man and woman is inclusive and descriptive of his entire being. This is the essence of what man and woman is.[9] Biblical humanism is based upon the revelation of the image of God in man. The wonderful, marvellous creation of man and the image of God is marred because of his fall due to disobedience.

The fall of man brought about a curse to the whole creation. Man was cursed and chased out of the Garden of Eden but the image of God was not removed from him; instead it was disfigured. Thus, he became a victim of foes and avengers. Man moves from the closest relationship of God to the world at large. Human being today is viewed as sick, weak and diseased, but not dead. The dark and depressing realities that human beings face are the effects of the primeval fall of mankind. A modern person, even modern Christian, does not seem to take this seriously. The fall of man was more than a stain, or blemish. It was complete and utter revolt against the person of God as revealed by His sovereignty, supremacy, authority and will. John Murray said that the *fall* was an assault upon the divine majesty and repudiation of his sovereignty and authority and a doubt of his goodness; it was a dispute with his wisdom, misuse of his freedom and, a contradiction of his veracity.[10] Man's arrogant desire for autonomy from God was an act of rebellion against the Creator's authority and benevolence that has caused havoc. The curse that resulted "affected not only man's spiritual relationship with God and his personal and social relationships, but also his whole economic and natural environment."[11] The results of this fall continue to astound us as we see so many young lives being ruined today.

Original man was seduced and tempted by the crafty and perverted creature, the serpent. It has not stopped there, it continues especially in these days. Many smart college students are seduced and tempted by the subtlety of the world and modernity; and they continue to increase their rebellion towards parents and society. This is the terrible result and the consequence of the fall of man. Man, after the fall, is no longer a creature of dignity bearing the real image of God but a marred image. The Bible gives a clear hope that despite man's rebellion he still bears the image of God. God in His great love did not annihilate man from the face of the earth but spared him to give him many more chances to realise his fallen and rebellious nature. For this God had to find the right solution, at the right time, to restore His relationship by building a bridge through Jesus Christ. R. Dingman, in his essay, "Fallen leaders are not damaged goods,"[12] argue that there can be reconciliation, restoration and dealing of broken relationships.

This can be accomplished only by the original maker Himself. Yes! Man is fallen and is unworthy of His grace, but God's longing heart for man whom He created does not allow Him to forget Him: instead He offered a grand plan of salvation to those who are most worthy. Even under the curse of sin and death, human still has dignity and bears the mark of his/her Maker. Wonderfully created, the crown of creation had a great fall which affected the whole universe in which we live today.

The awfulness of man's fall is balanced by the awesomeness of his image-bearing. The great depth of sin is matched by the great worth of man.[13] Therefore; God's grace does not reduce man to nothingness, but instead raises him to fellowship with his Creator. Irenaeus put it succinctly: "The glory of God is man fully alive." And a reformer stated a complimentary truth: "the glory of man is the living God."[14]

As Adam was conscious of his nakedness, today, in this age, we are aware of the nakedness of our nuclear madness, technological manipulation and the general depersonalisation, dehumanization of society which has resulted in various threats to life, such as; drug abuse, which is rapidly growing menace in our nation. In the dark and gloomy days such as ours, there is a ray of light – the hope in Christ. Humanity is still embraced and loved by God because He has invested His breath in human; Human beings are the instrument to carry out the mission of God. Hence, human is the image of God, he/she has dignity in them. With hope in God, they are nearer to God and can converse with God. But having these privileges he lost them by his doubt and disobedience. Yet he bears the marks of the Maker, he is not completely eliminated from the record and the heart of God. For God has made a covenant with him to be faithful and follow Him. Man is not only made in the image of God, a partner in covenant, but he is also a steward of God. God chose man with a specific purpose. Man with dignity has purpose and meaning in life and service. Today, young people are lost in the world but are still searching for meaning and purpose in life without knowing what they are searching for.

Steward of his body

God made human a steward of his/her body and life bestowed with dignity by the Creator. And he/she is to be a steward of their own life which is wonderfully and marvellously formed:

> For you created my inmost being: you knit me together in my Mother's womb. I praise you because I am fearfully and Wonderfully made: your works are wonderful, I know that Full well. My frame was not hidden from you when I was made in the secret place. When I was woven together in the depth of the earth, your eyes saw my unformed body. All the days Ordained for me were written in your book before one of them came to be.
>
> (Psalm139:13-16)

We have been made, crafted from conception by His marvellous care and wisdom. He wants human to take care of the formed body without abusing it. A steward is not the owner, but a manager, under the authority, whoever it may be. A steward acts and performs according to the direction of the owner. Human is a steward of nature, he is to keep it, tend it, protect and preserve it, but man with his selfish desire to satisfy his own life abuses the ecology. If one analyses carefully the drugs that are abused among college students and others, they are from plant origin – derivatives of a plant, but synthesised with chemicals. Some are straight plants like cannabis. Human beings, down through the centuries, have proved to be a poor stewards; they have failed to act within a given power; instead, they have gone far ahead which has ultimately destroying us and the creation of God. Yet God, in His goodness, has proved faithful to humanity's unfaithfulness. Humanity as a whole deserves death in Adam's sin, but God made a way out to have eternal life in Christ Jesus who is the model man. Pilate said, "Behold the man" (John 19:5). Jesus Christ is *the perfect*, real, model man, spotless and blameless, from whom each human being should draw his standards for his own life.

The Gospel of Luke 16:1-8 describes a dishonest steward. Here our concern is not to deal with the wider concept of stewardship but to emphasise that man is a steward of his own body and not the owner. Most fail to realise this, that we are only stewards and not the masters. Because of the fallen nature of human being, we forget the dignity given in God's image. We claim that we can do anything with ourselves. Who is there to question us? The rebellious nature of Adam, our forefather, continues in increased measure from one generation to the other.

But the idea that man is a steward of God in his relation to the world and his own life is inherent in the creation story (Genesis 1-3) in which he is appointed Lord of all things, except himself.[15] He is a steward of the gracious gifts that are bestowed upon him and he is to use them for the welfare of society and to glorify God, the Creator. Stewardship is to recognise that all gifts come from God and must be used for His glory as it is cited earlier, and this applies equally to all types of gifts, whether it is with money, time, talent or life.[16] Human being is not only a steward of life and nature, but also he is a dwelling place of God, the Creator, because all life comes as a gift. Our physical life, we just receive it. Spiritual life is "the gift of God" (Romans 6:23).[17] This gift is obtained and accepted, not attained. Human being has no authority on life and death, for it is a wonderful act of God.

Man is a Temple of God

Paul is emphatic on this theme in his Epistle to Romans and I Corinthians, as he says:

> Don't you know that you yourselves are God's temple and that God's spirit lives in you? If anyone destroys God's temple, God will destroy him; for God's temple is sacred, and *you are that Temple.*
>
> (I Corinthians 3:16-17)

And in I Corinthians 6:10-20, "do you not know that your body is a temple of the Holy Spirit, who is in you ... you are not of your own: you were bought at a price. Therefore, *honour God with your body.*" Human being can become saint with God, and without Him he/she can become a great sinner before God and humanity. We are not the master of our lives but sheathed with all beauty, talents, power and glory, nothing we own, for everything is given. God wants us to be holy, pure in heart, with a renewed mind (Romans 12:1).

God's prime concern is human beings and their life, whole purpose of God coming into this world as man to give life and that life, in abundance.

God never intends that any one should perish but has eternal life which He offers freely to them that come with penitent heart. The heart of human being is the throne of God. But young people even a whole generation has defiled that throne by indulging in unpleasant activities of the world. Students in search of kicks, or thrills, needlessly fill poison into their wonderful bodies, taken in the form of drug. This grieves the heart of the Maker. But His promise is if anyone defiles his/her body, scriptures encourage us to have cleansing from every defilement of flesh and spirit, perfecting holiness in God's fear (II Cor.7:1b). However, God gave the leaves of trees for medicines to relieve body pains ..." Their fruit will serve for food and their leaves for healing" (Ezek 47:12b). "And the leaves of the tree are for the healing of the nations" (Rev 22:2). So, one is free to use plants but not to abuse them to the extent of harming oneself.

Abusing the body is sin against God, since it is His throne and dwelling place. We prefer to live in a posh house, modern and clean, if human beings who are sinners by birth can aspire for such cleanliness, how much more the Creator of the universe, and the holy maker of human beings should He expect? Thus, to cleanse human being He had to shed His blood on the cross, to wash thoroughly and purify him, thus reconciling human beings to Himself. Above all, Christ bought us by His own shed blood, to have a new relationship with Him. He does not want His own to be enslaved to anything other than truth about God. God wants to redeem fallen humanity in Christ Jesus. But we continue to rebel against the divine call and the free gift of eternal life.

God did not create us without a particular plan and purpose. He had a definite purpose in making us which is to make us an instrument of His communication, revelation and the redemptive power of His mission. We are called to do the will of God, but He yielded to temptation of Satan and his loyalty and love for God was split. Divided loyalty or love is no loyalty or love: faithfulness to the truth gives him more credibility than anything else. They have chosen the easy way without realising the end. Proverbs puts it very clearly that "there is a way which seems right to a man, but its end is the way of death. Even in laughter, the heart is sad and the end of joy is grief" (Proverbs 14:12-13).

Life on earth is not the end, there is much more to live after this life. But our modern generation seems to have misunderstood the destiny of life, if this was not the case they will not act the way they do. So far the discussion has been focussed on man, his origin, quality, purpose and meaning in life. Our duty to God and human beings as well as our relationship with God and nature is what we infer from the Bible. If this is the picture of human beings painted on the pages of the Bible, then what should we say about our generation – especially of modern students? Where did they get the picture of life and its purpose? From whom did they learn this distorted meaning of life? Where did they go wrong? Or did we go wrong in educating, and passing on our moral principles & disciplines to our generations? Today's world has everything they need yet they go in for such substances, which kill them. Why? What has gone wrong with our society as a whole, that our youngsters need drugs? What do they gain at the end of the day? Destruction and death!

We saw that God created us in a perfect fashion, but the devastating fall marred the beauty and image of God. Yet God continues His relationship through the Covenant and through His Messengers/Prophets. Finally, He sent His own begotten Son-Jesus Christ, the Innocent One, who died for the whole world. The author's interview with many people revealed that is the family which has failed to impress the truth and meaning of life on earth to young people at the early stages. Disharmony, strained relationships, too much freedom, not listening to the expressed needs of children, not understanding the transition stages in them, lack of spending time with them, non-acceptance of them, and many other reasons could be pointed out. Secondly, the Church, the Body of Christ, has failed in its teaching and by giving importance to and engaging them in religious activities. The Church has given a totally different picture of life which has led youth into frustration. As a result, they have gone to places where they are accepted and loved; peer groups, clubs and social gatherings have led today's students into drug abuse. They do not need this dirty stuff. Yet to escape the depression, poverty, frustration and discouragement in the family and the Church, and the fun made by the peer group, have led them to be hooked to drugs.

Therefore, human being has become a handicap that is difficult to overcome. His world has become a nervous one, encompassed by anxiety.[18] The true joy and life does not consist in plentitude of earthly possessions. "The sole wealth is therefore the wealth of the soul."[19] If one loses it, he loses forever. Basic teaching which is essential for children is neglected under the influence of Modernism/ Westernization. This does not mean westerners lack disciplining- that is not the point. We have copied things not realising the cultural, social and economic positions. We have not taught what is required at the early stages in life. Many families seem to claim that we have done our part, but children must do theirs. This is only a self-defence mechanism which is not willing to evaluate one's own failures instead of trying to resolve it, with love and understanding.

Double standards in the family, society, unequal distribution of economy, corruption, injustice and immoral life, all of these have caused them to rebel and revolt against the system by indulging in drug abuse and living in their own world. Is it the answer? No. But the real power which can transform the system as well the abusing generation is the power of God. Human being cannot by his own effort save himself/herself or escape the problems of corrupt world. God's divine power will be sufficient to deliver both cause and effect. Peter, in his Second Epistle, very vividly pictures how we can overcome the world's corruption:

> His divine power has given us everything we need for life and godliness through our knowledge of Him who called us by His own glory and goodness. Through these he has given us this very great and precious promise so that through them you may participate in the divine nature and escape

> the corruption in the world caused by evil desires. II Peter 1:3-4

Having seen human's status plainly; the following section will deal with the moral and ethical demands on the drug abuser as an individual – the key person in the framework of society.

Moral and Ethical Perspective

To understand both the moral and ethical terms clearly, each must be defined in order to distinguish between both and their relation and its relevance to human beings in the society. Especially in relation to human conduct and behaviour.

ETHICS

The word, ethic, is derived from the Greek word, *ethos*; ethos, a manner of life, conduct, custom or practice, as described by some noted ethicists.[20]

Ethics is a part of philosophy, the part that deals with moral good and evil. It is concerned with the philosophical study of man's conduct: ethics ask above everything else about the meaning and nature of moral good and evil. It causes human beings to know about moral good. A problem in ethics arises when it's meaning and nature is misunderstood.[21]

Ethics can be defined as the systematic study of human actions from the point of their rightness and wrongness, as means for the achievement of ultimate happiness.[22] It is the study of the process of this life. So ethics can be called as practical philosophy. Ethics is the practical normative science of the rightness and wrongness of human conduct as known by natural reason or ethics is the study of all good and of how it can be achieved.[23] Thus, ethics is human for its progressiveness in that it purifies the religious crude forms which are inculcated in human beings. On the other hand, social ethics is the study of questions of good and evil, right and wrong, obligation and prohibition, as these arise in a social context. Modern ethics is purely the philosophic ethic which approaches man's responsibility from what can be known by natural reason and respect, to temporal existence. Theological ethics deals with what may be gained from alleged insight of any given religious community as to this life, or that which is to come. Christian ethics is the Christian insights of theological ethics. It weighs man's moral obligations in the light of this distinctive revelation.[24] For generations, Christians have found directions for daily life in the records of Jesus and the occasional counsel of the apostles. There is good reason to believe that the Apostolic Church offered considerable moral training to converts, covering abstinence from old sins and pagan ways, steadfastness under persecution, the fostering of fellowship and submission to the leaders. Ethical norms in the family life, societal movements and to civil powers are described here by Peter, who writes:

> They will be paid back with harm for the harm they have done. Their idea of pleasure is to carouse in broad daylight. They are blots and blemishes, revelling in their pleasure while they feast with you. With eyes full of adultery, they never stop sinning: they seduce the unstable: they are experts in greed – an accursed brood; They have left the straightway and wandered off to follow the way of Balam, son of Beor, who loved the wages of wickedness. But, he was rebuked for this wrong doing by a donkey – a beast without speech – who spoke with a man's voice and restrained the prophet's madness (II Peter 2:13-16).

The exhortation is in the midst of this kind of situation, we are not to give up moral and ethical norms.

This is an overall view of what Ethics means in different contexts of religion. Ethics is a *praxiological* reflection on ethos or customs or traditions and presently prevailing situations. Ethics has a broad scope which cannot be explained here, but this touches only the major and relevant features.

Morals and ethics are closely related in many ways, yet distinctive from each other. The term, moral, is derived from the Latin word, *mos,* or, *moris,* genitive form. It was used by the Latin philosopher

Aurelius to name customary behaviour.[25] This corresponds very closely to the Greek term, ethos, which means the same. In their meaning very little difference is seen, but there is a distinction between morals and ethics. Morals refer to the individual's behaviour and societal behaviour according to traditional and existing customs.[26]

Morality is related closely to religion as in practice, if not in theory; it is an aspect of it. Some hold the position of saying morality is independent of religion, but this is distinctly modern. Immanuel Kant was the first one to advocate this position. Prior to him, Plato and Aristotle held this position too. Some viewed morality not only as autonomous, that it can and should conduct its work in independence of religion, but even stronger. It holds that ethics can perform the functions formerly assigned to religion.[27] Ethics places standards and rules of conduct, but morality appeals to conscience, reason or to some principle which includes thought. However, moral philosophy is different from moral theology, which is also called Christian Ethics. Social ethics, General ethics (Philosophical ethics) are quite different from Christian ethics because it is concerned with identifying and elucidating the principles that determine quality of human behaviour in the light of Biblical revelation. Whereas philosophical discipline of ethics relies upon the authority of reason and which can only call upon rational sanctions for moral failures. As it was said earlier moral theology appeals to the authority of revelation, specifically as found in the preaching and ministry of Jesus Christ.[28]

Hitherto the terms ethics and morality were discussed in a simpler way. As human beings in a society, we need some guiding principles for our day-to-day life. To decide what is right and wrong, we need a measuring rod that could be ethics. One is under ethical obligations as long as one is in a community. We have moral and ethical duties to perform, which probably starts at home and extends to society. Ethical standards are for the welfare of the community and even for one's self. Unfortunately, human being is not under compulsion to follow them yet he is obligated to observe them for the cause of unity, common purpose and action.

Human decisions can reach no further than the light of knowledge which he has of moral values. He/she cannot develop a virtue unless he/she has at least some reflex insight and knowledge of the value it endeavours to realise. "If orderliness, neatness, thriftiness, comradeship, godliness are not apprehended as values no corresponding virtue can develop."[29] Where understanding of these virtues is absent, responsibility will also be lacking. Absence of these values in our families, the basic unit of the society, and to teach children certain things that are good which therefore ought to be done, certain things are unnecessary, others are harmful and the rest are evil, so they ought to be shunned. This formation and cultivation of moral and ethical values in the lives of children is required, first of all, the acquisition of practical knowledge which is gained by history, the examples of low and high morality, the concrete situations, environment, new trends in modernity, the decline of traditional values, religion and ethics. However, there is a difference between the conceptual knowledge of the moral good and devoted, effectual love for the moral value. This does not come out of mere personal enthusiasm or excitement but from the depth of one's own heart that is committed to the truth to do good; come what may! Love for moral value is attained and fostered by the deepening and faithful pursuance of the right fundamental option of final triumph or a miserable end. The former will lead to growing love for good and the discovery of new values, while the latter will lead to moral decline.

We have a right to do good and respect life but needs to be restrained from destructive and disrespectful attitudes to life and community. Though we find it difficult at times to respect addicts, strangers, criminals and morons, yet they are human beings, persons with weak personalities. Though humans have all authority to correct and condemn the evil acts or deeds, but not the person. There is hope for such people to be restored to normalcy by the community learning to respect them, love and understand them with sincerity and concern. One of the major causes that have led college students into drug abuse is lack of love, respect and understanding by the family or community. Instead, they are looked down upon, ostracised, damned forever, but not accepted as persons. No doubt they have violated their bodies, broken ethical and religious bonds and standards, yet a holier-than-thou attitude is a hindrance to giving respect to the other persons. One needs to treat the other person irrespective of social strata, habits, behaviour and the present situation with love and concern. For ethics demands to render respect for the persons.[30] The reason being, first duty is to respect life which is given as a gift from God, the ultimate reality. This treatment of an individual should be based purely as a human person created by God. In other words, it should not be done with ulterior motives, a motive is not then a drive to action or something which moves to do something.[31] but the concern and love of Christ must lead to help the fallen students. The interest of redeeming addicts must arise out of regard for a person, deep concern and as an ethical bond and moral responsibility.

Some religious principles may advocate such action, such as a follower of Hinduism might do with selfish motives. For him, *dharma*, or the observation of it, is the basis of moral life. In its depth, *dharma*, may have profound theology, but when it boils down to practical life, one thinks that giving alms, helping fallen old man, or doing something good which satisfies him, and ultimately leads him to *moksha*, is the stimulus. But, unfortunately, the Hindu ethical thought has not been upon the idea of an over-ruling God, righteous in Himself, seeking righteousness of His people, and helping them to attain it, that the moral life has been grounded.[32] So Hindu ethics are deeply tinged with the belief in transmigration, according to the doctrine of *Karma,* actions or deeds, under which every act, whether good or bad, finds reward not only in heaven or hell, but innumerable other bodies from a god to an insect or plant, even a stone.[33]

From Brahman to the low grovelling *chandals*, this theory compels them to practice *karma-marga*, practice of religious good deeds, in order to express their love and faith in God and religion which is their *bhaktimarga*, the way of piety, faith and religion. As they continue to practice, they attain *jnana* through a *jnana-marga*, way of true knowledge. All of this is done in the world to get rid of the cycle of birth and life. But modern man, or a Hindu peasant, does not have this idea of transmigration of souls. They have a vague idea of future life in which those who are good will be happy in heaven, *swarga,* while those who are bad will be wretched in hell, *naraka.* But in general ethics, this kind of attitude towards person and life is not promoted.

Islam emphasises that man is footstool of *Allah,* he decides whether man should be good or evil, in heaven or in hell. So man cannot improve by an ethical code, it is all decided by God. Each one understands life in different angles; therefore it is difficult in society to maintain a moral or ethical code. Many Muslim nations today are the ones who are involved in the drug business for there is no such rule in the Quran that goes against this. Mohammed, the founder of Islam, himself was a businessman. The question of morality does not arise while indulging in acts as long as they follow five foundations. One of them is *Zakat,* almsgiving.... a means of purification from his sins.[34] Some of the awkward behaviour is well accepted in this religion, however, our intention here is to say that because of this man is given low respect on the whole.

On the other hand, Christianity looks at man as God does. He is a created being, has potential for doing extraordinary things, sometimes good or even bad. He is the image of God, but the fall of original man affected the whole world and himself. But that does not end there; God has prepared a way for his redemption in Christ Jesus in which he is free to choose to accept or to reject it. Human being is considered the highest of all creation, little less than God, but not God. He is an instrument of God's mission which he has to carry out in this world. Though a sinner, he has hope of restoration and reconciliation in God. Human being has a high dignity in the sight of God as compared to other religious views and philosophies. For this he is commanded to follow the ethics or morals of God. Christian ethics basically deals with man and what he should desire and what he ought to avoid. What he ought and ought not to do; in Christian ethics conscience plays a dominant role to guide person's life pattern. Hence the end of Christian virtue is to be a perfect human being in Christ, to live with a sure hold of the world values which God has revealed through Christ, and to convert these values into reality. Ideal to all these actions is to make eternal life of Christ known to a sinner, so that he may experience it. Christians have a duty to themselves and to individuals because an individual is of infinite value in Christianity.[35] The group of believers who make the Church are to guard the freedom of man, and also they help their brother walk straight by wise counsel and love, always considering the other better than themselves.

So far the bare description of ethical and moral standards found in different religions and philosophies have been discussed. How then, do they have a binding effect on an individual and the society? According to the description given, each major religion and philosophy has ethical teachings, despite that there are numerous unethical standards and practices incorporated. How is that? It seems that the self, of every man, dominates humanities more than the set standards today. Each one wants to achieve something in life at the cost of the other person. It is a pleasure-oriented philosophy than a religion. People seem to be forgetting the temporality of life and existence. Ethical teachings and moral demands are pushed aside and each one has autonomy over ethical standards, whether for good or bad is not the concern. If everyone formulates their own moral standards for their own end and behaves as they please, they will not be beneficial to the community as a whole. For it will bring chaotic problems not only to the community but to the society in general. Prevailing situations of a nation can easily be traced back to laxity of laws, neglecting of moral and ethical standards, lack of respect for a person and, life. Selfish motives have led our country into corruption, the insanity of drug abuse, immorality, crime, and smuggling, exploiting, oppressing and seducing the poor innocent young girls, poverty, begging and increase in prostitution. The remedy for these consequences is to start settling and stabilising the centre of gravity, which is a small unit, the family. Government or society cannot intervene in personal affairs in many cases, but if each family can take care of their children's upbringing, in all accepted mannerisms, behavioural conduct and moral conduct, things could happen.

If drug abuse has become a threat to humanity, it is mostly the deteriorating familial and societal values that seemed have been the cause. From several interviewees, it was found out that young people have gone for that kind of habit in order to be accepted and loved within their peer group outside the family. *The family must become a church, temple or mosque to each child as it grows in that particular religious atmosphere.* It should inculcate the faith of its own against the dangerous, insinuation of modernity and attractions of the ultra modern world. The freedom and the independence given students have gone in for this unhealthy habit. Most of them long to get rid of it but withdrawal is very painful and even death may occur if it is done under careless supervision.

Society is good in pointing out the obvious misdeeds of these modern students, but fail to realise who would have caused them to be as they are now? What are the factors that allowed them to be hooked onto this poisonous substance? From where did they get this? (The how of it is dealt with already in the Second Chapter). Society wants to raise its financial standard by indulging in wrong business which harm its own fellow human beings. These poisonous, unnecessary, non-synthetic and synthetic drugs are killing thousands per annum in Indian alone, while an estimated hundred-thousand all over the world. Who cares for them? Ethics of these drug productions, involvement in coordinating and selling in clandestine ways, the exporting and importing of contraband dangerous stuff, and introducing drugs to school children or to post-graduate students. All this is with a vested interest to make money. Thousands of lives are claimed each year because of people who are concerned more about business than about ethics of any kind. Why do they do what they are doing? It is simple to analyse; by introducing some innocent people to drugs, those involved in it, including high officials, do so to amass wealth. It is all for personal gain. They are indifferent to the damage caused to many innocent people. The damage is such that it causes physical handicap, financial strain and eventual death. Then who is respecting whom? Who is working for whose welfare, what does one's personal ethics say? Is it not man killing man for his own selfish pleasure/gain? All that was said earlier boils down to this, that we have used the ethical autonomy, religious and social freedom, for our own ends. Drug abuse is not the result of one's own moral failure. The whole country, with all its governance, is accountable to this menace. Lawrence Fernandes, the Mayor of Bangalore City on 11 December, 1987 at the Seminar on Drug Abuse conducted by the Young Men's Christian Association, Student Christian movement of India, and in collaboration with other organisations, said, "I am sorry to say that even upper hands are involved in this drug business which is difficult to control, so we need to start a movement to voice our concern against this corruption and drug menace to appeal to the centre to take serious action against the drug business and its producers."[36]

At the outset we may accuse the drug abuser or an addict as a member of society, religion and even grade them as the greatest sinners, anti-social, hopeless outcaste and doomed to death. But God never has a measuring rod to grade each one's sin, for all are equal and sinners by birth in His sight and have to give an account of ourselves even for failing to remind the drug addict about the consequences. Ezekiel the prophet says:

> When I say to a wicked man," You will surely die," and you do not warn him or speak out to dissuade him from his evil ways in order to save his life, the wicked man will die for his sin, and I will hold you accountable for his blood.
>
> (Ezekiel 3:18)

What a demanding statement? We are indeed accountable and responsible for infusing both ethical and moral standards and saving the youth and the nation from the drug menace.

To pass judgement, condemn somebody else and blame the environment or circumstances is like the good old story in Genesis. God will not do that because man is His creation. If God treats us in this way, as we treat drug addicts, where will we be? We must stop talking about the situation and get down to that level of bringing solutions and rectifying the problems which is required of each member of a given society.

In my initial research, I was surprised to find out who were the ones susceptible to lured into drug addiction. Given below is a list of those categories of people and students who fall prey to drugs:

Affluent students tend to experiment with drugs more than those who come from lower socio-economic strata of the population.

Drug Users are economically dependent.

Most of them are students, ranging from school children to postgraduates.

Newcomers to colleges/university are more likely to use drugs: they get hooked specially through ragging.

Teens to twenty-one years are more crucial period in developing the habit of drugs.

English medium and convent school students are more than Non-English medium and other college students.

Students living in hostels form a higher percentage than those living with parents and relatives.

Academic frustration has led a few to use drugs.

Drug use is more among urban students than rural people.[37]

Why they are taken

For recreation, to seek pleasure, excitement, sensation and to escape problems
To cope with problems and difficulties of the society
To forget the pains and sorrow of poverty
Desire for acceptance and adventure
To rebel against the systems in society or those in authority

The factors that lead them to Drugs

Family which has not played an important model role but had strained relationships
Peer group pressure and acceptance
Identity crises in society
Environmental influence
To enlarge understanding and intellectual perception and life's ambitions
Poverty frustrations
Broken relationships and rejection
Lack of love and sympathy
Loose living and double standards at home
Poor discipline within and without

If these are the conditioning factors, what must be done to those hooked on drugs? We have discussed about the ethical and moral responsibilities of a family, the community and individuals themselves who are involved in trying to save addicts without having a negative attitude.

Drug addicts must be treated with as any other diseased persons who need medical treatment, psychological and spiritual as well.[38] There is no room to judge them but only to accept them as they are and give them moral and spiritual support. One cannot compare life to any material things. By doing this sanctity of life and sanctity of truth may be maintained in the community and in personal life. Christ Jesus loves everyone equally, there is no East and West, no addict and saint in Him. He gave His life to redeem every human being. Many addicts today long for deliverance from this menace and slavery. Unfortunately society has looked upon them as someone less than a human being. But Christ came to seek such people and we are commanded to love them and correct them by the truth. Thereby, they will understand the meaning and the ultimate destiny of human life's journey. Life is not just fun and excitement, it is much more than that, it is precious and one cannot afford to lose it. Jesus laid ethical foundations to those who follow Him; there is a great joy and hope in following His instructions. Christ never harbours the wickedness and impolite attitude of the drug addict or abuser, but he loves them all.

Drug abusers have failed in the beginning itself by resisting the insinuation of excitement through drugs. God's promise is "resist the devil and he shall flee from you." These weakling students have been carried away somehow or the other, therefore it is no point in talking of drugs as evil, but to take evaluative measures to prevent, if possible root out, this menace. It is not going to help anyone in any way, since it is a killer disease. We need to fight against it, eradicate it, with a war footing. One cannot take indifferent stand saying that, "it is not my concern." Today it is the neighbour's child who becomes a victim tomorrow is anybody's guess. The danger of drug menace is awaiting us at our doorstep. **Protect the member and prevent the menace.** Never hide the snake: it only bites you: chase it and kill it to maintain moral and ethical security and sanctity.

Listen to the cry of an addict

> Frequently I suffered separation from the family members I loved. The peer group were those I did not really love, but for pressure. Loss of wealth also came on me, it drained the family economy.... ignominies [sic], dishonour, full of affliction from police officials and likewise from the community, excessively poignant pain, both mental and physical. I also underwent frightful indignities of parents and fierce deaths and captivities of addiction. I had fallen into the hell and torments in the house of the withdrawal.[39]

Does this scene make us feel guilty of dereliction of our moral and ethical responsibilities? Does it quicken our conscience to reach the heart of people? Is there any listening to this cry? The Scriptural exhortation to "do good to all men"[40] is repeated throughout the Bible. Therefore, "whatever you do in word or deed, do everything in the name of the Lord Jesus ...."(Gal. 3:17). Hence we have social, ethical, moral and spiritual responsibilities to all human beings. A noteworthy point is that "failure to do positive good is a sin."[41] Let this challenge every right thinking person to do well, and to be positive in one's deeds. If the Lord is willing to forgive the addict, who are we to accuse them? Of course the Bible does not say Christ will forgive wilful disobedience and revolt by indulging in drug abuse. The Bible definitely condemns drug abuse or bad habits of any kind but not the addict or abuser. After all, a student who is an addict is created in God's own image so God forgives: "I will forgive their wickedness and will remember their sins no more." (Jeremiah 31:34b). God's transforming power can redeem anyone, so each must be a channel of that healing power that'll both ethical and moral fallenness. "Fallen leaders (students) are not damaged goods."[42] Because they are still the Creation of God, and hope to be transformed and healed in Him. These restored people can be effective students through a detoxification process. The truth remains, be scripture, moral and ethical standards does not condone any kind of abuse more so our bodies with wrong substances. Drug abuse is deplorable habit yet God loves the victim of addiction. Therefore, we have a responsibility as a community, Church, and as a society, to create an awareness and involve in preventive measures. The next chapter will deal with the practical aspects of the subject.

End Notes

1. Trueblood, *Life*, back cover.
2. O. S. Guinness, *The Dust of Death* (Downers Grove: Inter-Varsity Press, 1973), p. 273.
3. Ronald B Allen, *The Majesty of Man* (Portland: Multnomah Press, 1984), p. 13.
4. *Ibid.*, p. 66.
5. *Evangelical Dictionary of Theology*, s.v. "Steward," by F. L. Fisher.
6. Allen, *Majesty*, p. 12.
7. Edmond Jacob, *Theology of Old Testament* (New York: Harper and Row, 1958), p. 152.
8. Dietrich Bonhoeffer, *Creation and Fall* (New York: Macmillan, 1959), p. 36.
9. Allen, *Majesty*, p. 93.
10. John Murray, "Collected Writings", Vol. 2, *Select Lectures in Systematic Theology* (London: Benner of Truth Trust, 1977), p. 70.

11. Christopher J. H. Wright, *An Eye for an Eye: The Place of O.T. Ethics Today* (Downers Grove: IVP, 1983), p. 71.
12. Robert Dingman, "Fallen Leaders are not damaged goods," *Christianity Today*, Vol. 31, No. 18, December 11 1987, p. 12.
13. Allen, *Majesty*, p. 107.
14. Donald G. Bloesch, *The Future of Evangelical Christianity* (New York: Doubleday, 1983), pp. 19-20.
15. *Evangelical Dictionary*, s.v. "Steward."
16. *Ibid.*
17. Unknown Christian, *How to live a Victorious Life* (Grand Rapids: Zondervan, 1962), p. 65.
18. Cory, *Quotations*, p. 229.
19. *Evangelical Dictionary*, "Steward."
20. Walter C. Kaiser, Jr., *Toward Old Testament Ethics* (Grand Rapids: Zondervan Academic Books, 1983), p.2.
21. Leo R. Ward, *Ethics: A College Text* (London: Harper and Row Publishing, 1965), p. 4.
22. Vernon J Bourke, *Ethics* (New York: The Macmillan Co., 1955), p. 4.
23. Ward, *Ethics*, p. 19.
24. *Evangelical Dictionary*, s.v. "Ethics"
25. Bourke, *Ethics*, p.5.
26. J. T. K. Daniel and Gopalan R (Eds), *A Vision for India Tomorrow: Explorations in Social Ethics* (Madras: M.C.C., 1984), p. 158.
    Bourke, Ethics, p. 5
    Evangelical Dictionary, s.v. "Ethics."
    Bourke, Ethics, p. 5
27. *A Christian Dictionary of Ethics*, s.v. "Ethics."
28. *Encyclopaedia Britannica* (Micropedia), s.v. "Ethics"
29. C. Henry Peschke, *Christian Ethics* (Bangalore: Theological Publications India, 1981), p. 274.
30. Ward, *Ethics*, p. 290.
31. John Dewey, *Theory of the Moral Life* (New Delhi: Wiley Eastern Private Ltd., 1967), p. 154.
32. Shivesh Chandra Thakur, *Christian and Hindu Ethics* (London: George Allen and Unwin Ltd., 1969), p. 58.
33. *Encyclopedia of Religion and Ethics*, s.v. "Hindu Ethics and Morality," by Donald Mackenzie.
34. E. H. Palmer, *The Quran*, Vol. 9 (Delhi: Motilal Banarsidas, 1977), p. 308.
35. *Encyclopaedia of Religion and Ethics*, s.v. "Christian Ethics and Morality," by J Jelly.
36. Lawrence Fernandes, "Drug Abuse Seminar," by YMCA. SCM India and others, 11 December, 1987 at Bangalore.

37. Kenneth J. Lawton (ed.). *The Christian Response to Alcohol and Drug Problem,* (Bangalore: Ecumenical Christian Centre, 1983),
38. C. M. Francia, "Some Myths about Drugs and their Use, "*Health Action*, Vol. I, No.11, November 1988, p. 33.
39. Interview with F. Raju, a twenty-five year old Medical student of the city college, Bangalore, on 18 November 1987.
40. Geisler, *Ethics,* p. 182.
41. Christopher J. H. Wright, *Living as the People of God* (Downers Grove: IVP, 1983), p. 205.
42. Robert Dingman, "Fallen Leaders," p. 12.

Chapter 5

Missional and Therapeutic Implications

God's Missional plans began the day human being rebelled and sinned against Him. When He saw man's fall, He posed a question, "Adam, where are you?" (Gen 3:9). This seeking God, continued His mission of liberating fallen humankind through covenants, election and the call of His people. This mission of God was fulfilled in Jesus Christ whom He sent down to earth to seek and to save that which was lost (Lk.19:10). He did not send His Son to condemn the sinner but to liberate them from his/her bondage. The God of the Bible is a missionary God who sent His only begotten son to be God's Missionary on this planet earth. Therefore, "the Bible in its totality ascribes only one intention of God: to save humankind."[1] His intention to save is not limited to any particular Sect or a group of people rather it embraces the whole of humanity in His sovereign plan of redemption bringing salvation unto eternal life. Today, somehow or the other, the mission of God the Father, Son and the Holy Spirit continues through the Church of Jesus Christ in the world. George W. Peters says, "Mission is the total Biblical assignment of the Church of Jesus Christ."[2] The mission of God is for the people and by the people under the direction of a Triune God.

What is mission then? The word, mission, comes from the Latin word, *mitto*, I send; a synonym for Apostle, which is a Greek word, *apostello*, I send. Hence, an apostle or a missionary is a sent one.[3] Donald McGavran says, "Mission is God's programme for man." Thus, the Church is a missionary agent for change. The Christian mission is confronting error and proclaiming the good news about Jesus Christ in the power of the Holy Spirit, in the hope that the hearer will be convicted, confused and rebuked concerning his/her sin, and will repent and turn to faith in God through Christ.[4] Mission then is both the Gospel witness to all men and women, and the Gospel welcomes to fellowship in the name of Christ.[5] On the other hand, whether human beings repent and turn to Him or not, the heart of God goes after every creature whom He has created to seek and to save for His glory. This could be the summary of God's mission to humanity. God's mission embraces evangelisation to seek and to convince the sinner with the proclamation of the good news about the risen Christ and His free gift of salvation to the whole world. This is the responsibility of a changed person to an unchanged humanity in society and his stewardship is as part of his ecological concern. Since God is the Creator, Sustainer and Protector of the Universe, His mission does not exclude anything that is created or formed by His divine power. Bruce Nicholis defines, Mission, as a more holistic understanding of mission in terms of evangelism, church planting, caring for all who suffer (drug addicts and abusers included) a programme for the prophetic rebuke of the evil and injustice in one's society.[6]

The word, mission, is properly a comprehensive word, embracing everything which God sends His people into the world to do. It therefore, includes evangelism and social responsibility as well, since both are authentic expressions of the Love which longs to serve human beings in their needs.[7] So Christ sends His people – the Church – into the world to be its salt, to be its light. Mat 5:13-16. Having this holistic view of mission in mind, the drug addict or an abuser is in the universal plan of salvation, he is not cut off: that is not God's intention. God's mission is inclusive of drug abusers as well. God cannot look at him/her as the society or world looks at them. God loves them, not their learnt habits or activities. They are not god-forsaken people, for they are reachable and teachable. The mission of Christ is to embrace both sinner and saint so the Church is commanded to do the same without condemning the fallen human being. Though fallen, yet they have the potential to become saints in the sight of God.

The above-discussion clearly has the far-reaching implications for the mission of the church which in turn has a greater role to play in the lives of drug abusers and addicts in rehabilitating and restoring them to normalcy. It is not easy though, for it will demand much of our precious time, energy and money; it is worth investing in the interest of saving one person from clutches of subtle killer drugs for Christ's sake.

Mission of the Church and the Addict

Here, the issue is looked at from the theological perspective of the Church and its Missional functions in the light of God's mission through the Church, *an agent for change*. The study of Church, its constitution, ordnances and activities, such as work and worship is in itself a vast field of studies. Venturing into voluminous material on ecclesiology is not the focus of this section. Instead it is limited to Missional nature of the Church in relation to young students' struggle with drug addiction and enslavement. Concern here is the Church and its mission, evangelism and social responsibility in the world, as a change agent. For the sake reader, I have touched upon the doctrine of the Church, to show its relationship to drug abuse.

The term, Church, finds its nearest neighbour and sister in the Scotch term - *kirk*, and next to that, its cousin in the German, kirche.[8] In Greek, it is *ekklesia*, derived from *ek*, out; and *kaleo*, to call; denoting in good Greek usage, the assembly of citizens when called out from their homes to gathering places for the discussion of public business.[9] The word *Ekklesia*, came to mean, in a general sense, a gathering or assembly of people. Later in the Septuagint, and in the New Testament, it usually means, assembly or congregation, In Hebrew it is, *qahal*, congregation or collective community. In other words, it is people who are called out to be sent into the world to carry out the task of the Lord who is the head. The Church is the people of God, the Body of Christ, whose allegiance is to Christ, who are committed to serve Him in the world.

In the light of the above, we can define the Church as a body of persons called out of the world, and separated from sin by the power of God to faith in a crucified and risen Christ, having had wrought in them by the Spirit and through the Word, the nature of the risen Christ, being indwelt by the Spirit, made members to one another to serve Christ and men/women on earth.[10] Peter Kusmic defines "the church as that community which God gathers by the Holy Spirit to his own people and which is to be sent into the world to announce and to live out the message of the King who is the Lord Jesus. It is the company of men and women who by the very nature of their special calling are distinctively people of God, grounded in the redemptive purpose of the Church and who are determined by this special relationship between God and His people, Christ and the Church."[11] However, the Church is not the whole world but it is in the world to be light and salt. If the Church embraces the entire world and becomes universal, probably it would cease to be a Church or a called out company. Therefore, the church is a community of faith, committed to Jesus as Saviour and Lord; a community in which the Bible as God's word is the rule of faith and practice; a community existing to reconcile man/woman to God through the Gospel, and to nurture Christians to grow in faith and practice according to what God intended them to be. It is a community united on essentials, tolerant in areas of individual freedom, welded together in LOVE. Indeed the Church is also called to live here in the midst of the world; where its ministry is threefold: it ministers to God in worship, to the saints to nurture, and to the world as witness.

The Gospel call is a call to worship, to turn from sin and call upon the name of the Lord. The Church in any city is composed of those who call upon the name of the Lord in that place. According to Peter, the Church is God's own possession, so that "you may declare the praises of Him who called you out of darkness into His wonderful light."(I Pet.2:9). The Church, then, is a new nation under God, and the bonds that unite it are God-given.[13] So they (Church), in turn must not only love the Lord their God with heart and soul, they must also love the Lord and their neighbour as themselves. They are called to emancipate their brothers and sisters (even the drug addicts), they must not hate them in their heart. The underlying motive for this respect and affection is the joy of sharing together in the redeeming power and love of God. The Psalmist put it eloquently, "I am a friend to all who fear you" (Psa 119:63). The New Testament teaching goes one step further to say, "love those who hate you and pray for those who persecute you." Thus, the Church looks upward, to God in worship, inward to edify with teaching and sound doctrine, and outward to the whole of humanity bearing witness to the Christ of faith and the Jesus of history.

While Jesus was on earth He rendered His service to both rich (Lk 19:1-10) and the poor (Lk.6:20), to the educated (Lk.14:1-6) and the uneducated (Matt. 11:25-26); to the rural population of Galilee (Mk. 1:14) and the urban residents of Jerusalem (Mtt.23: 37), to the healthy and the sick (Matt. 4:23); to the just and the unjust (Lk. 19:10). It could even be said that Jesus took the side of the poor (Lk 7:22), the hungry and those who are mournful (Lk 6:21) the burdened (Matt.11:29), the sick (Mk 3:1-6); sinners (Mk 2:17), tax collectors (Matt 11:19), and Samaritans breaking all the barriers of culture and caste (Lk 10:25-37).[14] His ministry was directed to all aspects of human affairs especially those who were deprived of their privileges and needed His help most. Nothing hindered Him reaching out to those who were neglected and rejected by the society of His time. His humility and spiritual power penetrated every heart so is the Church expected to follow the mission and the ministry of the Master today.

Jesus came to earth on a mission from the Father, so that He might gather the remnant flock, the people given to Him by the

Father (Lk. 12:32; Jn. 17:2, 10:27-29). He looks with compassion on the people as sheep, scattered without a shepherd. (Mt. 9:36). Jesus the good shepherd undertakes that task of gathering the sheep to fulfil the prophecy of Ezekiel 34:1ff. The Divine Shepherd would come to gather His flock and deliver them from the false shepherds. He came as the 'Sent' of the father; not simply to call the unfaithful stewards of God's kingdom to account, but also to summon sinners to the feast of the kingdom (Lk. 14:16-26). For the Gospel is the message of God's redeeming love in sending His own Son into the world. Those who understand that love will be driven to share it. They will not only rejoice to sit down with other redeemed sinners in heaven's feast, they will seek other sinners in Christ's name to call them home. As Christ was sent, so He sends them, and the dynamics of mission is the heart of the love of God.[15] Jesus said, "as the Father has sent me, even so I send you." (Jn. 20:21). Therefore it is evident that the world evangelism, or transforming the world is the imperative of the New Testament and the Supreme Aim and task of the Church. The Gospel must first be heralded among all the nations (Mk. 13:10). Sinners must be made aware of their status, and the hope of redemption from bondage and salvation unto eternal life must be proclaimed by the Church. Jesus laid down His life to accomplish the mission of His Father so is the Church called upon to do the ministry of sacrifice for the cause of Christ. As Archbishop William Temple said *the Church is the only cooperative society that exists for the benefit of non-members.*[16] It does not matter if it loses its life, in order to gain a soul for the Kingdom of God, thus it will be greatly rewarded. The world of evil works through human beings and the systems to produce hate, selfishness, greed, murder, violence and perversion. Evil opposes God. Christ and the Church, ought prevail on these challenges and carry on their mission for the lost world (Jn. 16:33). "It is the world of sinister powers against which the people of God or the Church must wrestle with" (Eph. 6:12).[17] *The chief function of the Church is to fight and not merely to maintain drill, target practice and dress parade within its barracks.* It is designed to be a spiritual army of conquest, engaged in an offensive warfare on a world scale, pressing the claims of Christ and assisting Him in achieving His glorious purpose for the whole human race. This is still the day of the church militant not with violence but with love; it is not the day of the Church at rest.[18]

The Church is not designed to be a reservoir, ever receiving and retaining for itself God's spiritual blessings, but rather, a conduit conveying them on and out to others everywhere. Its true mission was, is and must ever continue to be the same as its Lord's – *to seek and save the lost* – whether at home or in a distant land.[19] The Church is God's unique creation, the result of historical and natural processes. She is God's unique possession through Jesus Christ, and thus it is expected of her that she be designed for a unique purpose and mission. The mission and purpose of the Church is not exhausted in the general movements of history. She performs her mission in history, yet she finds her origin, sustenance, true purpose outside of and beyond history. She is in time, yet she is of eternity: she is for humans, yet she is of God.[20] This is both reality and mystery of the nature and task of the Church. While the church is human in appearance, she is superhuman in spirit and design. Her design, mission and task constitute her task.

Let me take you back to the basic question of why the Church? What is its responsibility to the world of drug abusers, which is rampant in our city and nation? To answer these questions, first, the Church exists to carry out Christ's great commission and purpose through liberative evangelism and edification of the weaklings. Secondly, if the Church is the people of God called out to minister to people, then its immediate and urgent responsibility is to deal with the number One enemy of India, the drug menace which is destroying the future and welfare of humanity in the whole world.

You might think that the author is sermonizing the issue at stake, the readers are free to draw their conclusions. The author's intention is not to philosophize the writing rather it is to get the message across the readers. What should the Church be doing in context such as this? The following text will help the readers in understanding the Church's involvement and commitment to fallen humankind. As it was noted earlier, the Church has a threefold responsibility: **to God, to self and to people outside the fold.** The Church which is not concerned about society is heading towards destruction by its own indulgence in non-profiting affairs like drug abuse and addiction. It is probably not as a wholesome Church which the Scriptures depict. It is not to be content with its members alone but extend its love and concern to those who are outside, under the rule and control of demonic powers. The work of evil forces is to influence people in such a way, that their true function in creation is brought to ruination.[21] Whereas the intent of God is to preserve His creation especially humankind who bear His image. Drug empire along with other evil forces is leading the whole world astray (Rev 12:9) through the means of drug-smuggling, trafficking and peddling, he is turning the human perception of reality into something other than what it is, causing people to be deluded and misinformed regarding truth about life, its purpose, sin and goal.[22] Therefore, the Church's mission should be confronting the drug menace and to address addiction, which is a serious problem. This should be its urgent concern.

The Church, as the called-out people of God, the fellowship of repentant and forgiven sinners, has the responsibility to carry the goodness of abundant life to all those who are ruining their lives with drugs. Jesus' ministry was to poor and the rich, sick and the healthy. His concern was the whole human being. So, the Church is to be concerned with the mind, the soul, and the body which is the temple of God and should be cared for. Christ's blood was shed to purify every member and help them lead a holy life which is expected of them. It has to be more concerned with addicts as sick people rather than sinners. Yes, he is a sinner no doubt, but one cannot cut him off from the main stream society. Christ who is the head of the Church still waits for an addict to return to Him. It is possible when the Church carries out its mission to save fallen humans and restore them to a fellowship; it is called to confront the destructive agencies against life such as drugs and addictive substances. Addiction in all its forms is against the purposes of creation, and so against the will of

God. In each addiction creation suffers, one must understand life is a gift from God and it is to be lived for His glory.

The Church should affirm each person as infinitely valuable and precious member of God's creation. In other words, the Church is an inclusive community. There is no room for excluding anyone. Persons (who are addicts) are to be accepted as human beings created in God's image, valued, loved and cared for in every way. The mission of the Church is to care for the drug abusers and addicts, not that we support them in their bad habits, but to help them to come out of that bondage with love and sympathy. Jesus cared for everyone, irrespective of caste, colour and creed, so it is the duty of the household of God to carry the legacy of the Master. Scriptures portray the Church as a body with many members, and if one member fails and falls into drugs, it affects the whole family, Church, society and nation. Hence, we are called to bear one another's burden and become a community of acceptance. The Church has a greater role to play in reaching out to drug addicts, conscientizing its members, creating awareness in the society about the adverse effects and the devastating end it brings. Thus, the Church being light can "get the light to shine in every dark corner of the world."[23] Especially, for those who are blinded by drugs.

Having recognised the burning problem and its rampant spread throughout the world, the Church has the responsibility of combating this destructive menace. The addiction destroys not only the individual but also the family, the community at various level, hence the Church's attitude can never be judgemental; instead be considerate, compassionate, constructive and reformative. The drugs are human products to serve their own end. The ramification of it is distortion of human personality, destroying God's image, and also human's tremendous potentiality.

The mission of the Church must focus on the burning issue to save young lives; it has to set its priority in order to deal with this dreadful problem more than any other issues including that of reaching the unreached. Overlooking the issue at hand will allow the menace spread like gangrene. The Church's mission must exercise its ministry of bringing life, hope and liberation to these unfortunate victims and their families. Drug abuse is not excluded from the mission of the Church; it is very much a part of its ministry. The Church's mission is to deplore evil and promote good in the world. Drug abuse and addiction should be condemned, deplored and deserves capital punishment. The addicts should be helped in all possible ways to return to normal life again. He is like a lost sheep and a fallen man on the wayside crying for help. Is the Church of Christ hearing?

The above discussed idea may be good, how then, should those things be put into practice to reach out the addicts wherever they are. For this the following section will discuss the practical aspects of the Church's mission. It is easier for anyone to present a well written paper, it is rather difficult to implement and practice it. Does the Church of Christ know what is happening in and around our country today? If it does, what is it doing to combat the drug menace?

If it is not aware of this rampant spread of drugs, which is published and broadcast all over in print and mass media almost every day, then there is something drastically wrong with the existing local church. We are feigning ignorance and deliberately plugging ears to the gravity of the drug menace. The possibilities of this sort of attitude may be because:

1. Church has lost its missionary vision for lost humanity
2. A lack of concern for the perishing young lives
3. Self-contentment and short sightedness
4. Poor understanding of human life
5. Lack of compassion and love for the suffering lot.

Where mission is attempted without compassion, the communion with God is lost.[24] Mission implies lostness and foundness that all are initially lost but that some will be found. Fundamentally there is a recognition that human is spiritually lost and dead, and unable to find his own way back to God, but those lost in the drug world should be reached by God's mission through the Church - the people of God.

Practical Suggestions

As discussed earlier, it is easier for experts and scholars to make extraordinary and tall claims to eradicate the drug problem in India. This is quite common with political leaders, seminar leaders, even organisations like the Narcotic Bureau, NGOs etc. The real question is who can bell the cat? That is the predicament that the Church and the Country suffers with.

Of course, addicts are rotten and beyond redemption one might think and he/she may be right in their own right. On the other hand, we are not too far behind them. We too are saved sinners; nobody can claim to be perfect except God on both realms. We concluded earlier that drug abusers and addicts are sinners and they need to be treated as the diseased persons. Quite a few interviewees revealed that they longed to be liberated with proper care and treatment, both medical and spiritual support is not available to them. A young man, in an interview, said, "my parents are well to do, so they took me to a doctor after detecting that I was an addict and treated me, but who will treat and care for slum dwellers and streetwalkers?" (This statement is made elsewhere in this book.) Asina of Bangalore, a teenage girl was talked about a lot but nothing happened to her personally till the Young Men's Christian Association (YMCA) reached out to her personally and treated her under Dr. Yusuf Merchant in Mumbai. Whatever was written about her in print media such as Newspapers and magazines did not help her.

Therefore, this Chapter suggests some practical methods to deal with drug addicts especially as part of the Church's mission. They are medical treatment, psychological treatment and spiritual treatment, which are essential ingredients of restoration, rehabilitation and de-addiction. The Church's mission for drug abusers and addicts is carried on through the above mentioned means or methods. While implementing them one or the other might lead an addict to restoration. Christians are recognized in the history as people of **the way** – the way of God, or way to life eternal.[25] Part of the Church's mission is to show people the true path of righteousness and the way to Christ. He is the way, the truth and the life. The

Church has to identify with the people's suffering and show her love for those who are deprived as a living witness to Christ. That is her mission on earth. Again and again, human being is driven to *nihilism* to the conviction that life is futile. It is God's purpose through His self-revelation to put an end to this futility. God's purpose is the redemption of human being,[26] through the community of people - the Church, His body. A "truly apostolic Church is a church engaged in mission,"[27] to drug addicts who are dying every day without the knowledge of the Lord Jesus. The Church is commanded to open confession and proclamation of Jesus in mission, to addicts and abusers. Therefore, Christ must be proclaimed to the addicts as a **great healer,** psychologically Christ as the supreme counsellor and spiritually as the wonderful and loving Redeemer from their bondage. If the addicts realize and seek help, they will receive His grace and restoration.

Medical Treatment

As an addict is a diseased person just as any other sick person, this is a fact which has to be kept in mind. Drug abuse is an illness of the soul-mind-body. It results in as well as psychological and as well psychological dependence, leading to spiritual deterioration. The saying, "once an addict, always an addict,"[28] can be disproved if an addict goes through proper medical treatment along with psychological and spiritual treatment.

If anyone comes to know that a family member, specially a student, is an abuser, or an addict, he/she must be taken to a good doctor for treatment. There is no room for accusation, manhandling, gossip and ostracism; in case this is done to an addict, it will aggravate the problem instead of eliminating it. A lovable, respectable person can become rebellious, hostile and defiant towards everyone. Because of this, medical personnel advise to treat an abuser as a sick person but not as an outcaste of the family, community and the society. Some go to the other extreme of hiding their children's misbehaviour especially, drug abuse in order to protect their familial honour in the society. True but it does not help either the parents, or the community. Both are unproductive methods such as making a big public scene about an abuser, or hiding the case is not going to help in any way. Knowing this kind of a situation, doctors plead the parents and community as a whole to take precautionary measures and seek early medical advice and treatment as soon as they spot their child on drugs.

When a drug abuser goes through medical treatment after a prolonged use of drugs, he/she enters into a traumatic experience called, withdrawal symptoms. Just as there are two types of drug dependence, there are two forms of withdrawal symptoms. If a person becomes physically ill, when he stops taking drugs, he may be considered as physically dependent. This is most obvious with narcotic substance users. Withdrawal results in severe physical symptoms including stomach and muscle pain, vomiting, diarrhoea, running nose and sleeplessness.[29] However, withdrawal if painful and dangerous, sometimes, addicts or abusers may die or even go back to their old habit, when a person undergoes withdrawal from hard drugs like brown sugar, without any medication or substitute drugs, the withdrawal symptoms are most severe and obvious. This type of withdrawal is called, **cold turkey**. Despite the trauma of such a withdrawal, it is the form preferred by addicts and social workers because the very trauma brings home to the addict the reality of dependence. Since a simple form of withdrawal is thought to be associated with a relapse, so the difficult period of cold turkey withdrawal is preferred, it often provides the addict, time to make a conscious decision to ensure that this break with the habit will be final.

The administration of medication to relieve the withdrawal symptoms should be the primary concern of trained medical staff. Otherwise sudden withdrawal, as noted earlier, can prove dangerous, even fatal. Detoxification and medication being complete should be undertaken gradually under the supervision of a specialist. On the other hand, it can amount to a waste of time, money and energy of the well-wishers, family and the doctor.[30] However, the Church being the agent of God's mission for change, its members must be patient and willing to forego anything in order to save the life of a youth no matter what it costs. It only happens when Christian doctors and medical workers commit themselves for this cause as partners in the mission of Christ. Due to lack of commitment to this cause, as of now, there is no known medical or psychiatric care that can place any claim to high success rate in curing addiction.[31] Though there are quite a few rehabilitation centres and homes that have come up in the recent past. I have had close connections with few of them run by christian individuals and organizations.

We cannot blame medicos or counsellors for not having high success in revitalising an addict as a normal person. Partly, or mainly, it depends on the addict whether he/she is willing to be restored or wishes to remain under the clutches of drugs. Any treatment of addiction can only succeed if the addict has a genuine will to be reformed and perseveres in cooperation with the treatment.[32] If addicts undergo detoxification and medication willingly in a hospital, they will feel better and begin to see a change both in physical and mental thought process. Addicts start regaining lost health and the intensity and frequency of his/her craving begins to recede gradually, at least for the time being.[33] Hospitalisation helps only in catering the physical injuries and illness, the more complex psychological issues are mostly left untouched as the proceeding discussion may make things clearer.

Therefore, early detection is important to start early treatment for the abusers. Once a person gets dependent on a drug, it is very difficult to revitalise him/her. However, they need to go through a detoxification process. What is detoxification? Detoxification is mainly to control the withdrawal symptoms and it is actually removing a toxic or poison from the body by letting them into the experience of cold turkey. Patients must be admitted to a psychiatric ward and the substance which is abused be stopped completely.[34]

In the case of treatment failing, relapse can occur in an addict. Doctors suggest that they can administer anti addictive substance, but it is not the best method. Weaning the addict away from drugs is not easy, yet efforts must be made to reintegrate the former addicts and fallen students back into society. Christian medical institutions and services can be different from that of Government or private agencies. Medical institutions are established in India to treat the poor and the needy. Today, our medical treatment can bring change in the addicts' physical and spiritual being. As in Bangalore a girl who was given some kind of treatment by different people, but nothing happened. YMCA General Secretary, Mumbai, said: "we tried to reach Asina, a chronic abuser, with love, concern and sympathy. She was brought into our clinic and given Christ's love and care. At the end Asina said, the place is different, you are different, I feel totally different here than at any other hospital. Why is that? If this is the testimony about the Christian treatment and care, the Church of Christ must pursue its mission to drug abusers through medication. Medical aid for addicts should be part of the Church's mission because Christ Himself was involved in healing ministry of both physical and mental diseases.

Psychological Treatment

"For lack of guidance a nation falls, but many advisers make victory sure" (Proverbs 11:14).

Medical treatment alone is not complete to revitalise and restore addicts to normalcy. In order to succeed in this treatment, the basic cause for which the person had turned to the drugs in the first place has to be looked into. If only the psychological defect is removed to regain his/her self esteem, can the desire from drugs and the risk of relapse be eliminated?[35] How a Church can involve in the psychological treatment as a part of the its mission. There are numerous psychological factors which have been the cause for students to go in for drugs. Unless causes are dealt with, and clarified, rehabilitation is not possible. Psychological problems are complex, and they need specialised treatment and care. There are now quite a few psychotherapy centres in India. Mostly these are located in Delhi, Mumbai, Goa, and Chennai and in Bangalore. As compared to the increasing menace, these centres are inadequate and ill-equipped to, handle the enormity of the drug problems. Therefore, it is a challenge to the Church of Christ to set up counselling centres and even rehabilitation centres to deal with psychological problems as part of the local church's Missional wing. Very few Protestants, or believers, have taken keen interest in setting up a counselling centres, or day care centres to rehabilitate drug addicts. One of the senior pastor's wife in Bangalore had set up a day care centre to deal with primary stage issues related to addictions.

There are few leading churches like Methodist Church at Richmond Town, and the CSI Church at Lingarajapuram, which are involved in counselling service. The latter is specifically dealing with drug problems.

According to available statistics, Bangalore had about forty to fifty thousand addicts and many more abusers in 1987. Can one CSI church project be a gate way to combat with the rapidly increasing problem? The question is, what are the existing local churches doing with regard to the drug menace and for the youth of the Church and Society? To who is their ministry directed? Look at what the Scriptures says: Jesus answered, "Those who are well have no need of a physician, but those who are sick: I have come not to call the righteous, but sinners to repentance" (Luke 6:3-32). The prevailing situations in the churches imply that, its ministry is directed towards those who are well than to those that are sick and dying. The author is in no way saying that we must not serve others except drug addicts; our ministry must have priorities like that of Jesus. Of course, there are various kinds of addicts apart from substance abusers in the Church – sex addicts, alcohol addicts, money addicts, position and power addicts etc., also those that are professing Christ with lips need to be reminded of the heart-warming experience and spiritual awakening. On the other hand, focus of Church's ministry should be extended to drug abusers and addicts who are heading towards destruction both physically and spiritually.

There is a tremendous need for setting up counselling and psychotherapeutic centres in each local church to deal with human problems. Sunday's ministry is not enough to meet the prevailing drug problems. Drug addiction is not a simple matter of physical dependence. It is a manifestation of a longstanding personality problem that has many forms; addiction is one of the symptoms. Detoxification and cure of the desire for drugs has little effect on underlying pathological personality problems, only one manifestation of which an abuser was pushed towards drugs intake.[36]

The unanswered question, "Who , or What, am I?"[37] Who am I? Needs clarification in the minds of the students through the ministry of psychotherapy and counselling. The feelings for recognition are challenged and threatened by modern science which seems to say that human is basically a machine or a mechanism. We, as thinking human beings are treated to be no more than a machinery of atoms.[38] Therefore, ministry of psychology and counselling helps our young people to see and to understand the worth and value of life, as well as dignity and majesty of human beings in the light of Christ and the Bible. The feelings of rejection, depression, personality disorders and flaws have driven students into drugs. Treatment of psychology must help open their eyes to see reality, that they are not rejected rather accepted and they have potentiality to cope with the problems of the world and live meaningful life on earth. The church must accept them as addicts who long to be accepted, and help them to understand that drugs are not the answer to the problems, but Christ is the only answer for all practical problems revealed in His words (the Bible). The ministry of counselling needs careful approach to deal with addicts. Positive strokes should be given initially to ease them of tension and confusion. In turn, it helps counsellors, or a therapist, to build rapport and to gain confidence of addicts. As this takes place, it becomes easier to help addicts change their personality and relinquish their drug habit. Supportive suggestions and relationship play an important role to heal psychotic problems. A counselling ministry of the Church can do a lot of good than medication, because medication is to treat withdrawal symptoms which will be for a short period whereas psychological problems are complex and prolong for months together. Therefore, addicts need to be treated empathetically not as orthodox Christians who would say, "addicts are condemned sinners and beyond redemption." On the other hand, liberals take a neutral stand with regard to addiction. Both views are wrong, so there is a need, for a balanced understanding of the value of life.

The ministry of psychological counselling must aim at removing the underlying psychological reasons for addiction by bringing them to light and getting the addicts to accept life's situation, crises and face them head on.[39] It must also enable them to overcome their isolation, and loneliness by seeing the world objectively outside of themselves and identifying themselves to relate with fellow sufferers. Psychological malfunctions usually consist of, or stem from problems like guilt, anxiety, resentment, lack of self-acceptance, feelings of personal unworthiness, insecurity, wrong priorities and selfishness.[40]

Psychology helps us understand better the causes of human behaviour and malfunctions. While an addict is counselled, he/she begins to bounce his/her ideas and start thinking afresh of his/her attitude towards life and society. At this juncture, God's truth and purpose for life can become clearer and meaningful. This could motivate him/her to live a worthy life. Christian counselling reveals everything that we need to know to live effectively and is also found in scripture, either directly through teaching or indirectly through examples.[41] Many people may feel good while changing an addict's behaviour or circumstances through their counselling. The real change can occur when Christ renews his/her mind. The ministry of therapeutic counselling should encourage the discouraged feelings of an addict and help overcome them by feelings of joy, happiness and hope in Christ. Pastoral counselling will exhort to overcome evil behaviour or problems of behaviour in the light of Christ. Therefore, counselling must enlighten the troubled person like an addict to divert his/her mind from concentrating on their present crises and help them to focus on to the Biblical insights that problems are temporary and transitory. Those who go through the challenging situation in life will receive the final reward of eternal life and joy. Counsellors will have to empathise with painful feelings of an addict and help them to identify sinful behaviour patterns responsible for the negative emotions and manifestations in the society and to uncover the wrong thinking which led to the maladaptive and destructive behaviour.[42]

The pastoral counselling must make an addict understand that Christ will lead him/her into all truth - "You shall know the truth and the truth shall make you free" (John 8:32). The ultimate purpose is to liberate abusers from their abusive habits. At the end, an abuser should say, "I am transformed by the renewing of my mind in Christ:" that should be the primary goal and mission of therapeutic and Christian counselling. Addicts feel empty, meaningless, lost in the world of their own and for them no one seems to care.[43] Why do addicts see apathy and insensitivity in the general public, more so among the family members and Christian community? Probably the indifferent attitude of the people/community blindfolded them to see gravity of drug menace, particularly victims of drug addiction. The urgency for liberative and therapeutic care for suffering youth has not been understood in India. How then, can the Christian church along with psychotherapists render healing, caring service for those groping in a world of drugs?

Therapeutic approach of Jesus to sickness and other forms of human brokenness are the central motif in the New Testament. Daniel Day Williams makes this clear, "the language of salvation and the language of healing are interlaced throughout the Bible though the two are not identical."[44]

So, the Greek word, *therapeuo*, means both, to serve (a divinity) and, to care, to treat (medically), heal, restore back to normal health.[45] Is this the command of the Gospel for the body of Christ - the Church? Biblical images of the Church make abundantly clear that it is there to empower its mission. Central to biblical mission is healing, liberation [from drugs], spiritual nurture and empowering the weak for God's mission in the world. According to Paul Meaner there are more than 90 images of the Church such as the people of God (II Cor.6:16), a caring community united by a new covenant in Christ; the body of Christ (Rom 12:4-5; I Cor 10:17) etc. This is a unique unity in which each member, each part of the living body, has his or her special gifts and ministries. The ministry of reconciliation, liberation, healing, admonition, praying, supporting, encouraging, empowering, warning etc.[46] Jesus' paradigm for the mission of the Church today is – heal the broken hearted, seek and save the lost, love the unlovable, touch the untouchables [lepers, AIDS victims, addicts], reach out to the unreached and rejected, go beyond the borders to bring the lost into the fold of God. What is stated above should remind the Church of Christ (whole body of believers in Christ) here and everywhere that they should re-think their mission strategies to care for those crying aloud for help and get themselves involved in creating awareness programmes and assisting government of the day in eradicating the drug menace, that is the number one enemy of the nation.

Some Indian therapeutic counsellors and psychologists have suggested very effective ways to work with drug addicts through the church's ministry. One of the psychologists and therapeutic counsellors well respected in and out of India is Dr. B. J. Prasantham, who is at present directing Christian Counselling Centre, Vellore, Tamilnadu. His proposed counselling skills and methods that are found useful are:

- Rapport - building bridges with the client in order to earn his/her confidence, in other words, make friendship so as to enter his/her world troubles.
- Give physical and psychological attention, let them know that you are interested in them and wish to see them back to normalcy.
- Take initiative to deal with addicts, they may not open up to you, then counsellor must walk an extra mile.
- Empathy, respect, genuineness must be upper most in dealing with an addict, no room for condemnation. An addict must know that there is someone to care. That is the true nature of a counsellor.
- Advance empathy, confrontation, self disclosure if need be, and value clarification.
- Family and community needs to go through counselling process to rehabilitate the addits[47] Concerted efforts from

whole family and expression of support to victim can have lasting effect on his/her restoration.

Every Christian community and the society needs to follow some of the above mentioned suggestions to carry out the mission mandate. The Church's mission field at present is the world of drug abusers and addicts. This section of humanity needs to be reached out as they are looking for acceptance and rehabilitation. The holistic ministry of Jesus Christ is the commission to the Church:

> Many people (addicts) are looking for an ear that will listen. They do not find it among Christians, because Christians are talking when they should be listening. He who no longer Listens to the brother or sister will soon no longer be Listening to God either.[48]

Let this be a warning to each member of the community that suffers ignominy of drug addiction and a challenge to get back to Christ's model of ministry. This is not a theological debate but a practical assessment and a reality of the present churches in India. The Church should, assume responsibility for restoring, distressed and addicted people. Addicts are suffering from helplessness and ineffectiveness. They are crying out to be restored to full productive and joyful life. To achieve the mission mandate, the local churches must develop its own unique resources for therapeutic counselling. The Church must have strategies for mobilising and training counselling personnel according to their gifts from within the members to meet the needs of people. A member of the body can involve himself/herself in a meaningful and constructive ministry of helping one another. The Church must work together by putting all its efforts and talents to save these addicts who are succumbing to death almost every day without hope. However, medical and psychological treatment for addicts alone may not be complete if spiritual treatment is not considered here. The Church is not here merely to render social service, it is equally concerned with spiritual nurture of the individuals as well.

Spiritual Nurture

Spiritual nurture is the need of the hour for every ills of the society. More so the youth who have been enslaved by illicit drugs. Youth have resorted to drugs as a revolt against the system that has been indifferent to them. On the other hand, the whole of humanity is revolting against God and His standards by indulging in corrupt practices at all levels. For this very purpose the Incarnate Christ had to give His life on the Cross to liberate and restore fallen humanity. Despite His offer of salvation and free gift of eternal life, humankind continues and persists in sinful activities. The personal problems which plague so many always stem from this fallenness in human beings. In simple words, this is a result of failure to follow God's principles for living - missing the mark of God's intended spiritual and ethical standards.[49] As a free person, man chooses to do things that excite him and bring greater pleasure for a moment. God's purpose for human being is not a momentary excitement or temporary pleasure but eternal joy that lasts forever.

The Church on earth is an agent for spiritual nurture and care. It does not mean that it possesses all the required qualities of spiritual doctor instead acts under the direction of the Triune God. The Church is to live like Christ and show the world, in its lifestyle, that Christ offers forgiveness for those who repent of their sins of all kinds including drug addiction.

The Church therefore, is under solemn obligation to do the following:

- To present Christ vividly, intelligently, attractively, effectively and persuasively to the world and to an addicted individual as the Saviour of the World, Sovereign Lord of the Universe, and the coming Judge of all humankind.
- To lead people into faith relationship with Jesus Christ in order that they might experience forgiveness of sins and newness of life. Human being must have salvation experience which, in turn, should bring change in his habits and heart

if he/she is to inherit eternal life and eternal fellowship with God.

- To establish believers in Christian doctrines, principles and practices of Christian living, Christian fellowship and service.
- To train them in a life of the Holy Spirit, since the Christian life is charged with supernatural ideals and demands.[50]
- The Church is a reconciling agent between fallen human beings and God. Reconciliation is a change of relationship between persons; God and human: person and person (the peer group that led him to drugs).
- The Church is the agent of forgiveness, liberation and restoration.

How should the Church treat those abusers, addicts, murders, corrupt, wicked, perverted and fallen? The answer should be like that of Christ: "I came to seek and to save sinners".

- The God we worship is both infinitely holy and infinitely loving. Therefore, He demands that humans made in His image be not only holy but also loving, gracious and forgiving. This is perhaps the heart of the problem. We tend to be with those who are of our nature and well-respected in society, but condemn addicts and fallen people. If God of the Bible encompasses both sinner and saint, so must we.
- Christians are sinner-redeemed, but still sinners; tempted, prone to sin and actually sinning, yet we judge, condemn each other especially drug abusers and addicts as somebody eternally condemned. But for the grace of God we too could have been condemned lot, if not one among them.
- God is disposed to restore the fallen. His goal is to restore everyone to perfect Christ-likeness.[51]
- Genuine forgiveness does not necessarily imply restoration to high position. It only implies we should seek to restore who has been hooked on drugs to usefulness, not leave him

> as damaged goods, that is, to be thrown out as rotten veggies or garbage.

The Church of Jesus Christ is an independent body. Ultimately, we are dependent upon God, in the Church the brotherhood of believers and fellowship of believers are responsible for one another including perishing addicts. God holds the Church responsible for the spiritual deterioration of those who are dying in sin without knowing or hearing about God's love, who accepts everyone alike. We, as the household of God, are responsible to lead students into a true confession. We are also accountable for their sinful life, for sin is never an isolated act. We, who are sensitive Christians, should seek to bring about reconciliation with God and restoration to an abundant life. The Church will be stronger when we take more seriously what the Bible has to say about how we should treat those who have fallen to drugs and are leading a perverted life. God's word has clear teaching that Christians should help addicts by extending to them all the reconciliation and restoration that accompany genuine forgiveness. That is what makes our faith so unique and attractive to the drug world.[52] The understanding of suffering, willingness to listen, expression of compassion ... these are in roads into an addict. Once they re-open their heart, then grace can enter. The love, empathy, spiritual & moral support, and liberation from the hell-like experience is what the addicts are longing for. Spiritual treatment of the Church can bring change in emotionally troubled students who have been on drugs. Restoration of an addict do cost person's time and reputation etc. One has to withstand accusation, insult and shame, for Christ's sake. Addicted students are longing to come out of that hell, but who can help them? Is the Church not the agent of God's mission to the world? A narrow understanding of the Church, and its functions, has belittled its universal character/nature. Here is a rehabilitated addict's testimony:

> How many years passed by, I cannot tell because each year was a worse hell than other ... ten - eleven years – and then one day a new manager walked into office and he got

> hooked to me (loved). For me it was a strange experience to be receiving love without having to pay for it in any way. And I found that my conscience, long since dead, had begun to wake up again. I began to feel ashamed of my lifestyle. I began to feel unclean and unworthy.[53]

Is there such a Church around us to extend a compassionate love, care and concern for the addicts?

As air, water and sunshine are essential for the body; hope and trust in a Supreme Being (God) is essential for the soul. If the soul is healthy, the body will also be healthy. Everybody has to find meaning in life as the Scriptures reveal it to be, otherwise there will not be any motivation to life. Therefore, personal contact and encounter with God through Church ministry, or friends and personal prayers, will instil hope, purpose and meaning in life. **With God there is endless hope, without God it is a hopeless end.**[54] How true is this saying in the lives of addicts? The Church has the great commission to live as God's ambassadors in the world, as well as torch bearers to pass on its spiritual heritage to those who are outside the fold. We must take note of Paul's exhortation here: "be careful how you live. Don't live like ignorant people, but as wise people ... Don't be fools, then. But try to find out what the Lord wants you to do."[55] Hence, the serenity of prayer is the quintessence of what the Church must seek to do.

> God, grant me (us) the serenity to accept the things I/We cannot change, the courage to change things I/we can and the wisdom to know the difference.[56]

So, then, the Church cannot take the easy road and neglect to do good to the needy.

In summery the thoughts discussed so far, such as: medical treatment will revitalise the broken and crushed student addict. The treatment of the mind will rehabilitate and uplift the fallen student addict. But treatment by the Master (Christ/Church) will restore an empty-hearted student addict to spirituality, joy and happiness in Christ. All this is possible as the Church carries out its Missional service based on the great commission of Christ. While Christians, therefore, do not have ready-made answers to all moral, ethical and spiritual problems, they at least have a firm starting point. They can offer forgiveness, love, care, acceptance and concern which they themselves have experienced in Christ. Hence, let the Church resolve to commit themselves as the household of God to serve Him and humanity by making this classic prayer of Francis de Assisi:

> Lord make me a channel of thy peace that where there is hatred, I may bring love – that where there is wrong, I may bring the spirit of forgiveness – that where there is discord, I bring harmony, that where there is error, I/we may bring truth .... that where there is despair I may bring hope, that where there is sadness, I may bring Joy. Lord, grant that I may seek rather to comfort than to be comforted – to understand than to be understood – to love than to be loved. It is by self forgetting that one finds. It is by forgiving that one is forgiven. It is by doing that one awakens to eternal life.[54]

Therefore, the Church is to engage in Healing, Sustaining, Guiding, Reconciling and Nurturing people of God especially the victims of drug addiction. The Church may make use of Spiritual resources such as scriptures, prayers, worship services, fellowships, rituals and sacraments effectively.

Christian Strategies for Dealing with Drug Abuse

Individual Level

- Educating an individual is essential to deal with drug abuse. One need to know what drug abuse is? How is it done? Who are prone to indulge? Why do they indulge? What are the effects and symptoms? Their life-style and so on, should be known to an individual who intends to involve in such a service.

    ☞ *The pastor* must know about the drug world as the shepherd of the flock; i.e., his own local church. He must possess extra discerning powers to detect drug abuse among his own church youth and deal with them. He must educate himself in counselling skills, and modern trends, like drug abuse among college students. He must learn their behavioural pattern and if he finds such cases, who are contacted then he must know, how to deal with them initially? He must educate himself about the drug menace by reading the daily newspapers, journals, magazines and books written by Indian authors as well as western.

- ☞ *Youth workers* must go through training under reputed counsellors, especially those who are dealing with addicts. So far, we do not have any training centres for the drug world. However, seminars, conferences are frequently held in our country. Such seminars, conferences supply much needed information. Youth workers should educate themselves with all the information to deal with youth who are a prey to the drug menace.
- ☞ *Laymen* must know what is happening among the youth/student world. A pastor's teaching in the church alone will not solve the problem but there should be a corporate effort to fight against this menace. Therefore, individual persons must be educated about the drug world.

Literature, seminar papers and counselling centres which deal with drug abuse will be good educative information for each responsible individual.

Teaching: having learnt about drug abuse, these trained lay people are to teach people on the personal level without over-sensationalising or glamorising the drug scene, instead its bad effects on mind, soul and body as well on the family, society should be made clear.

Laymen must teach at home, his family members and neighbours. Pastors should use pulpit ministry to educate their congregations, youth worker to youth generation. Addiction will finally result in death, incurable diseases, mental illness, but not its initial euphoric experiences. So, it is important to educate oneself and educate others about drug abuse. Each one must know the causative factors which lead students to drug abuse. One must deal with the cause before dealing with addiction.

- Creating awareness in the immediate context and neighbourhood by conducting seminars, talks and discussion of the prevailing menace and preventing one's own kith and kin from this danger. Once people understand the seriousness of problems related to drugs they will be more willing to help in preventing the emergance of related issues by detecting cases early and helping addicts to recover.
- Strengthening each family to provide love, acceptance and Christian nurture, giving help to build self-esteem of each person, student and child. Keep open the communication channels and uphold higher moral, ethical and spiritual values in life.
- The Church being a larger family should enrich and encourage the functioning of individual families, where family values are strengthened and reinforced. Opportunities for expression, entertainment, mental health and emotional maturity should be offered to any local church. Help the youth to develop resistance to temptation and will power to make better choices and responsible use of freedom.[58]
- Involve students and youth in creative activity, religious and social activity in order to keep them busy so that they may not go in for bad habits like drugs. As it is said an "empty head is a devil's workshop." Sunday school, youth activity, prayer meetings, Bible study, retreats, camps, conferences, tournaments, excursions, hiking, hunting, sport and games, rallies, parties, etc., are suggested religious and social activities for the Church to execute and practice for the benefit of saving students and youth.
- Teach each child early in life about the value of life, and purpose of living, for we are only stewards of life and

body; not owners. Teaching patterns must be like that of Deut 6:7:

> And you shall teach them (commandments) diligently to your children, And shall talk of them when you sit in your house, and when you walk by the way, and when you lie down, and when you rise."

And Proverbs 13:20 "He who walks with wise men becomes wise, but Companion of fools suffer harm.

- Reach out to vulnerable groups or addicts through schools, colleges and organisations. Prepare and distribute literature on the subject of drugs and collect stories of recovered addicts and abusers, their conversions and new life in Christ should be published in Church journals, bulletins and any other Church-related publications.
- Develop new and innovative resources like counselling units, medical units, rehabilitation centres for the help of addicts and their families. To discover and to develop their abilities and use of internal strength, to direct their lives.
- Work to identify the cause for these students' aggression, rebellion and their de-meaning attitude towards self and society.
- Help and encourage these students learn to forgive those who have hurt them and to forgive themselves in order to increase their self-esteem[59] and to know that they are precious and valuable human beings.
- Accept and involve these students in all activities at home, community, fellowship groups for who they are, not for what they do. Respect them, make them feel at home, share God's love, healing and redeeming power. Let students and youth know that you love and value them.
- Help those students and youth to know that life is not simply excitement and fun, but it has to go through innovations, difficulties, struggles with great hope of eternal life and

reward. Teach them to learn to live with problems, stresses, pains as God's grace enables them to live with it.

- As members of the larger community of faith, we need to recognise our own limits and know when we fail. To deal adequately with addicts, we need to refer these students to competent professional help. While we continue to nurture and support these young people with our acceptance and support.

Community Level (*Networking with other expertise*)

Locating and identifying the help and resources outside the church to help these addicts to work with them.

- Training: Recruit volunteers from different professions and age groups and train them in:
  - Providing necessary counselling skills, attitudes to drug abuse and how to understand them.
  - Develop Biblical perspectives and spiritual resources to encounter and to restore them.
  - Provide clear information about what drugs are all about and its defiant effects on an addicts' language.
- Be informed and value the work among addicts outside the church. If possible, give your support and suggestions for effective work and definite co operation with governmental and non-governmental agencies to combat the drug menace.
- Encourage Government and police vigilance with your positive co operation to fight with the complexities of drug trafficking and its abuse more vigorously and strategically.

Hold consultative meetings with those who are involved in this kind of work to refer to them when complex problems arise. The Church and its community dealing with addicts will approach them through the heart of Christ, unlike rest of the society's dealings which are more on the physical and psychological level. If the household of God adapts these strategies with God being their help, they can bring about a great change and prevent drug menace and save the society and the nation.

Theologically trained pastors and qualified theological educators have had their children encounter this menace personally. Drug menace does not spare any one, can attack anybody, and before it strikes one must take precaution and prevent it happening to any human being.

End Notes

1. George W Peters, *A Biblical Theology of Mission* (Chicago: Moody Press, 1981), p. 9.
2. *Ibid.*, p. 11.
3. Robert Hall Gover, *The Bible Basis of Mission*, (Los Angeles: Bible House of Los Angeles, 1946), p. 26.
4. Peter Cotterel, *The Eleventh Commandment* (Downers Grove: IVP, 1981), pp. 17-18.
5. David Brainard Woodward, *God, Man and Mission* (Glendale: Gospel Light Publications, 1964), pp. 6-7.
6. S. D. Ponraj, "Theological Education for the Church and its Mission," (M.Th. thesis, Bangalore: SAIACS. 1988), p. 10
7. John Stott, *Christian Mission in Modern World* (Bombay Gospel Literature Service, 1978), p. 15.
8. Emery H. Bancroft, *Christian Theology* (Grand Rapids: Zondervan Publications, 1976), p. 282.
9. *Ibid.*, p. 283
10. *Ibid.*, p. 289.
11. Bruce Nicholis, (ed.) *The Church: God's Agent for Change* (Exeter: The Paternoster Press, 1986), p. 67.
12. Joe S Ellis, *The Church on Purpose* (Cincinnati: Standard Publishing, 1982), p. 22.
13. Donald A Carson (ed.) *The Church in the Bible and the World* (Exeter: The Paternoster Press, 1987), p. 35.
14. Gerhard Lohfink, *Jesus and Community* (London: ISPCK, 1985), p. 89.
15. Carson, *The Church*, p. 46.
16. John Stott, *Issues Facing Christians Today* (Bombay: Gospel Literature Service, 1987), p. 24.
17. Robert K. Webber, *The Church in the World* (Grand Rapids: Academic Books, Zondervan, 1986), p. 16.

18. Glover, *The Bible Basis*, pp. 34-35.
19. *Ibid.*, p. 34.
20. Peters, *A Biblical Theology*, p. 208.
21. Webber, *The Church in the World*, p. 17.
22. *Ibid.*
23. Glover, *The Bible*, p. 37.
24. Cotterell, *The Eleventh*, p. 21.
25. *Ibid.*, p. 32.
26. *Ibid.*, p. 44.
27. *Ibid.*, p. 41.
28. Alice Orasta, "Drug Abuse – Counselling Drug Addicts," *Health Action*, Vol. I, No.11, November 1988, p. 29.
29. O'Toole, *Drugs and Youth*, p. 37.
30. Narayanan, "Can Drug Addiction Be Cured?" *Mirror*, April 1988, p. 23.
31. *Ibid.*
32. *Ibid.*
33. Lobo, *Drug Addiction*, p. 121.
34. Abraham Varghese, "Drug Abuse among the Adolescent" an updated paper, p. 7.
35. Narayanan, "Can drug ...." p. 24.
36. Jyoti Mishra, "Counselling Drug Dependents," *Health Action*, p. 27.
37. Colin Chapman, *The Case for Christianity* (Harts: Lion Publishing, 1981), p. 13.
38. *Ibid.*
39. Stanley Coelho, "Drug Addiction and Counselling for Social Change" (n.p & n.d.), p. 4.
40. Lawrence J Crabb, Jr., *Effective Biblical Counselling* (Grand Rapids: Ministry Resources Library, Zondervan, 1977), p. 34.
41. *Ibid.*, p. 41.
42. *Ibid.*, p. 183.
43. Howard Clinebell, *Basic Types of Pastoral Care and Counselling* (Nashville: Abingdon Press, 1984), p. 46.
44. *Ibid.*, p. 61.
45. *Ibid.*
46. *Ibid.*, p. 65.
47. B. J. Prashantham, paper presented at Indo Asian Workshop on Drug Abuse Control, New Delhi, India, 10-12 September 1987.
48. Dietrich Bonhoeffer, *Life Together* (New York: Harper And Bros., 1959), pp. 97-98.
49. Crabb, *Effective*, p. 41.
50. Peters, *Theology*, p. 213.

51. Kenneth S Kantzer. "The Road to Restoration," *Christianity Today*, Vol. 31, No. 17, November 20, 1987, p. 20.
52. Dingman, "Fallen leaders..." p. 12
53. Patricia Palaparti, "Special Report," *Health Action*, Vol. I, No. 11, November 1987.
54. Alice Crasta, "Drug Abuse," *Health Action*. p. 33.
55. Colin, *Christianity*, p. 46.
56. Narayanan, "Can Drug ...." p. 25.
57. Lobo, Drug Addiction, p. 134.
58. J. D. Solomon, "Alcoholism and Drug addiction – the Church's Responsibility," *The South India Churchman*, August 1987, p. 9.
59. Olson, *Why Teenagers*, p. 212f.

Conclusion

Drug menace is no new challenge to our country and our Church in particular. It has been there since 1980s. While the problem may not be as bad as in some other countries, it is certainly not as one wishes to think of this issue at hand. The media has its own agenda and are more concerned about their TRP rather than presenting the serious issues confronting the nation and its youth. It is clear from the evidence provided in this work that the menace is certainly worse, and far more pervasive in our society, than perhaps we have hitherto been willing to admit. *Times of India Pune* edition on 15 and 19 January 2016 highlighted gravity of Drug menace.

From the Therapeutic and Missiological point of view, it is understood that drug addicts are in fact a group of needy people as much as any unreached peoples group to the mission of the Church. One cannot afford to treat them as discarded cases and hopeless people for whom nothing could be done. Many addicts are terribly degenerate in their behaviour and attitude toward society and religion due to apathy and insensitivity of the public towards them. God who created them is not in such haste to discard and disown them. Instead He has long patience and gives the addict a chance to return to His love and care as the father in the parable of the lost son was waiting to embrace his prodigal child.

It is proved beyond doubt that the drug malady is dangerous and dreadful. It is claiming many young lives that have ended up with an imaginary world leaving aside the reality of life. They are not in a position to face the bare facts of life, and the world. Many college students are crying aloud for help – "is there anybody listening?" "Can anybody help us out of this hell and restore us to normal life?" Some had to end up with disastrous death, without knowing the reality or experiencing the beauty of life. And some are longing to escape from their sufferings but hardly any help is being extended to them. Despite witnessing this drug menace, Government authorities seem to be quite helpless to bring about a lasting remedy. This kind of attitude calls for Christians to awake and contribute their best to liberate and bring those lives who have lost their way in the world of drugs. Situation is grim and if not attended at war footing by the government of the day, it will worsen the future of the youth, the hope of the nation.

The book is in no way painting the nation in bad light rather stating the facts and figures based on various input and available information. Governments of the states and the centre together must fight this battle in one accord without indulging in petty politics of blame game. Nevertheless, the author who has grown up with young students exhorts every Indian citizen to be involved in fighting against this gigantic battle of drug abuse. According to the statistics mentioned in this book, every second student of any college has tempered with or been confronted by the issue of drug use. This kind of abuse and drug-dependence has increased crimes, robbery, incurable diseases like AIDS (Acquired Immune Deficiency Syndrome) and STD (Sexually transformed diseases), homosexuality and many more undiagnosed diseases which are killing young lives. Can anyone who knows the value of life keep quiet and put up with this kind of grave situation? The author feels that this kind of attitude is detrimental to the society. Everyone who knows the truth must arise and open his or her eyes to see the decaying world and extend his/her loving, caring and supporting hand, to rescue those who are susceptible to the multiplicity of factors that lead to, or induced into drug abuse.

The drug menace in India has caused economic imbalance and instability in its development. Some unscrupulous and selfish men have amassed wealth and have become drug lords claiming many young lives in course of their drug business. It has created fear and uneasiness among parents. Many are panic stricken to see the tragedy among students who are expected to be the future leaders of the nation but too often the hopes and bright future plans that they have dreamt for them seemed thwarted. Is there any solution for people and students who are going towards, or through, the crises of uncertainty, confusion, threat of life, dark and gloomy periods? Yes! The author has stated in summary some suggestive measures which may help prevent this drug malady, if not, at least decrease the rapid spread of the drug market and smuggling from both the Golden Crescent and the Golden Triangle. This will surely help the country in so many ways to concentrate its personnel and channel its resources to much more productive projects than the unproductive and destructive drug menace. It is not only the Government's concern but every single citizen has a responsibility at individual and corporate level to address this issue and participate in this invisible war raged against youth of the Nation.

Having said so much about drug malady and its consequences, at various levels, this book has encouraging and positive strokes that even though a student is an addict, yet he has a bright future and hope in Christ Jesus, the saviour of the world. Therefore, the Church and secular agencies are addressed very strongly and positively to wake up and be aware of this issue. We can no more afford to say that our child is safe and the problem is not ours. In fact, this drug devil is waiting to devour. The mission of the Church is to focus on this needy group of people who are trapped in this horrible pit. God sees them as fallen ones and wants that they be liberated, saved and reconciled to the fellowship of His chosen people.

Addicts need love, care, concern and forgiveness from the almighty God, whom He is willing to forgive and accept as they are. Who are we to deny that which belongs to Him? Hence we are commanded to love one another as He loved us, and by doing this we obey His commandment and so, in turn, we will fulfil His purpose in our lives on earth. Let us hope that the Lord will give the heart of forgiveness and accept the fallen such as drug abusers. Let us ask God to give a heart that is full of compassion for those unfortunately or inadvertently caught up in such debasing habits.

It is accepted that all Christians may learn to recognise it as part of our responsibility in mission to involve ourselves in the lives of all those, including drug users, who have gone astray from the transforming grace of God.

Bibliography

Primary Sources

1. Communication (Mass Media)

Addicts Testimony, broadcast from Radio station, Bangalore, 7:30 pm. 10 November 1987

Singh, Swaran (Interviewer), "Is Anybody Listening." Video tape. Bombay: St Pauls's Communications. 1987.

T.V. programme on "Drug Addiction," NIMHANS staff. 6:30 pm. 20 May 1987.

2. Pamphlets/Tracts

"Delivered from Drugs". *Booklet.* Bombay: Gospel Literature Service. 1987.

"Drugs." *Tract.* Don Bosco Youth Animation, Bangalore. (In writer's possession)

"Is your Child a Drug Addict." *Leaflet.* Society for Prevention and Rehabilitation of Drug Addicts (SPARDA), Bangalore. (In writers possession)

3. Periodicals/Journals

Aikyatha. Nos.4-7. April 1987-July 1987.

Austin, Gregory A. (Ed). "National Institute on Drug Abuse." Issue No. 24; 1978.

Chitnis, Arun. "Hooked, You kick the Habit." *SUN,* Vol. IX, No. 48; 5 July 1986.

Christianity Today. Vol. 31. November 1987-December 1987.

Duncan, R. A. "Depression among Youth." *Our Link*. Vol. No.1. January-April 1985.

Govinda Rao, K. V. "Drugs." *Wisdom*; June 1988.

Health Action. Vol. I No. II, November 1988.

Hendricks, Howard G. "Parents Communicate Your Convictions." Light of Life; July 1987.

Indian Youth Care. Vol. I; July 1986-January 1987.

Kottary, Sailesh. "Busting the Mob." *The Illustrated Weekly of India*; 23 October 1988.

Lamb, Jonathan. "Drug Abuse." *Harvester*. Vol. LXV. No. 12; December 1986.

Mathew, P. D. (Ed.) "Ban Harmful Drugs and Tobacco Ads" *Legal News & Views*. Vol. II No. 8; August 1987.

Narayana, K. "Can Drug Addiction Be Cured?" *Mirror*; April 1988.

Nelson, Jacke (Ed). *NIDA, Research Terminology*. Issue 26; 1982.

Richard, Louise G. (Ed.) *NIDA Research Monograph* Series No. 35; 19 May 1981.

The South India Churchman; August 1987.

4. Newspapers

Deccan Herald (Bangalore); July 1987-December 1987.

"Give me Little Gard." *BLITZ*; 12 August 1987.

"Hooked on Slow Poison." *Current*; 13 June 1987.

Indian Express. (Bangalore); May 1986 - November 1987.

"Postscript." (Gard Ka Rasta). *The Indian Post*; 5 July 1987.

The City Tab; September-November 1988.

The Hindu. (Bangalore); June 1987 - January 1988.

The Times of India. (Bangalore); May 1987- December 1987.

5. Encyclopedias/Dictionaries

A Dictionary of Christian Ethics. 1981 ed. s.v. "Drug" "Stewardship" by John F Sleaman.

Collin's Dictionary of English language. s.v. "Society."

Dictionary of Islam. s.v. "Zakat."

Encyclopaedia of America. 1964 ed. s.v. "Drug" by Austin Smith.

Encyclopaedia Britannica. Vol.I. s.v. "Amphetamine" by John C. Ballin.

Encyclopaedia Britannica. Vol. V. s.v. "Cocaine."

Encyclopaedia Britannica. 15th ed. Macropedia. s.v." Drugs and Drug Action."

Encyclopaedia Britannica. Micropedia. s.v. "Moral Theology."

Encyclopaedia Britannica. Vol. 20. s.v. "Sociology" by Norris John Wats.

Encyclopaedia of Religion and Ethics. s.v. "Christian Ethics and Morality" by D. MacKenzie. "Hindu Ethics and Morality" by J. Jolly

Encyclopaedia of Social Sciences. s.v. "Drug addiction" by C. E. Terry.

Evangelical Dictionary of Theology. s.v. "Steward" by F. L. Fisher.

International Encyclopaedia of the Social Sciences. s.v. "Drug Addiction Social Aspect." J. A. Clausen. "Society."

Narramore, Clyde M. *Encyclopaedia of Psychological Problems*. Grand Rapids : Zondervan Publishing House. 1981.

The World Book of Encyclopaedia. s.v. "Drugs." K. L. Kaufmann.

6. Unpublished Documents

Channa Basavanna, S. M. et al. "Pattern and Problems of non-alcoholic drug dependence in Karnataka". Bangalore: NIMHANS. 1987.

"Delhi Foundation for Correction, De-Addiction and Rehabilitation." Delhi (details n.a.)

Verghese, Abraham. "Drug Abuse among the Adolescent." CMC Vellore. (details n.a.)

Coelho, Stanley (Fr.). "Drug Addiction and Counselling for Social Change." (details n.a.)

Ghosh, Mallike. A paper on, "Problem of Smack Addiction in India – Some Relevant Factors." (details n.a.).

Glory, Debhora. Random Notes on Drugs (details n.a.).

Mathews, Vikram. "Incidence Causes and Prevalence on Drug Abuse." (details n.a.).

Lokhandwala, Vilas. International Conference on Drug Awareness. 22-24 March, Bombay at Hotel Oberoi. 1988.

Mehara, Jyothi. Counselling Drug Dependents. New Delhi. ASHIANA Drug De-Addiction Centre, (details n.a.)

Kumar, Priya Sampath. "Personality Traits in Drug Abuse and Alcoholism" (details n.a.)

Ponraj, S. D. "Theological Education for the Church and Its Mission." M.Th. Thesis. Bangalore: South Asia Institute of Advanced Christian Studies. 1987.

Prashantham, B. J. Indo-Asian Workshop on Drug Abuse Control. New Delhi. Vigyan Bhavan. 10 -12 September 1987.

Singh, Hira. Drug Abuse: Prevention. New Delhi: National Institute of Social Defence. Ministry of Welfare. Government of India. (details n.a.)

7. Interviews

"A" Medical student, Bangalore. Interview. 27 November 1987.

Appiah, Prakash. St. John's Hospital and College. Bangalore. Interview. 20 December 1987.

"B" Engineering student, Bangalore. Interview. 28 November 1987.

Babu (pseudonym), Engineering student, Bangalore. Interview 25 November 1987.

"C" Medical student, Bangalore. Interview. 24 November 1987.

Channabasavanna, S. M. Dean and Professor of Psychiatry, NIMHANS, Bangalore Interview. 19 December 1987.

"D" Theological student, Bangalore. Interview. 16 November 1987.

Divyatha, Jyothi Nivas College student, Bangalore. Interview. 11 December 1987.

George, C. A. Peoples Education Society, College of Engineering, Mandya. Interview. 8 May 1987.

Kumar,V. Professor, NIMHANS, Bangalore. Interview. 13 May 1987.

Michael, Marcia. CMS Secretary, Bangalore. Interview. 7 December 1987.

Naik, Kasturi (pseudonym). Government official, Bangalore. 25 November, 1987.

Prathiba. 'Gate way,' Lingarajapuram, Bangalore. Interview 10 May 1987.

Pruthvi, YMCA student leader, Bangalore. Interview. 22 May 1987.

Puttu (pseudonym). Engineering student, Bangalore. Interview. 20 November 1987.

Rajshaker, Satish. Pharmacy student, Austin Town, Bangalore. Interview. 22 Janurary 1988.

Ramu, student of city college, Bangalore. Interview. 5 December 1987.

Thomas Asha, Mount Carmel College, Bangalore. Interview 11 December 1987.

Tom (pseudonym). Postgraduate student, Bangalore. Interview. 25 May 1987.

Williams, Suri. Area Director Y.F.C., Sri Lanka. Interview 12 June 1987.

Secondary Sources

Books

Adams, Jay E. *The Christian Counsellor's Manual.* Philadelphia: Presbyterian and Reformed Publishing House, 1983.

Aiyer, P. S. Siva Swamy. *Evolution of Hindu Moral Ideals.* Delhi:Glen Publishing House, 1986.

Allan, Ronald B. *The Majesty of Man*. Portland: Multinomah Press, 1983.

Bancroft, Emery M. *Christian Theology*. Grand Rapids: Academic Books Zondervan, 1976.

Baker, Don and Emery, Nester. *Depression*. Portland: Multinomah Press, 1983.

Banks, Robert. *Paul's Idea of Community*. Grand Rapids: Wm.B.Eerdmans, 1982.

Bloesch, Donald G. *The Future of Evangelical Christianity*. New York: Doubleday, 1983.

Bonhoeffer, Dietrich. *Creation and Fall.* New York: Macmillan, 1959.

__________ . *Life Together*. New York: Harper and Brothers, 1959.

Bourke, Vernon J. *Ethics*. New York: The Macmillan Co. 1955.

Bourne, Peter G. *Addiction*. London: Academic, 1974.

Brown, Robert McAfee. *The Significance of the Church*. Philadelphia: The Westminster Press, 1956.

Calkins, Raymond. *The Christian Church in the Modern World.* New York: The Macmillan Co., 1924.

Carson. D. A. (Ed.) *The Church in the Bible and the World.* Exeter: The Paternoster Press, 1987.

Clifford. Rawntree Paul. *The Mission of the Church*. London: SCM, 1951.

Clinebell, Howard. *Basic Types of Pastoral Care and Counselling.* Nashville: Abingdon Press, 1984.

Coder, Brica W. *Drug Abuse*. Iowa: William C. Brown, 1975.

Cohen, Sydney (Ed.) *Drug Abuse and Alcoholism*. New York: The Harworth Press, Inc. 1981.

Copestake, David R. *Cannabis: Is Hash Safe*? Exeter: The Paternoster Press, 1979.

__________ . *Is Hashish Safe*? New Delhi: Select, 1981.

Cory, Lloyd. *Quotable Quotations*. Wheaton: Victor Books, 1985.

Cotterell, Peter. *The Eleventh Commandment*. Downers Grove: Inter-Varsity Press, 1981.

Crabb, Lawrence, J. Jr., *Effective Biblical Counselling*. Grand Rapids: Ministry Resources Library, Zondervan 1977.

Daniel, J. T. K. and Gopalan R. (Eds.) *A Vision for India Tomorrow: Explorations in Social Ethics*. Madras: MCC, 1984.

Davis, John Jefferson. *Evangelical Ethics.* Grand Rapids: Baker Book House, 1985.

Dewey, John. *Theory of the Moral Life.* New Delhi: Wiley Eastern Private Ltd., 1967.

Domnitz, Myer. *A World of People Book One: Studies in Human Environment*. Oxford: The Religious Education Press, 1971.

Douma, J. Chrisitan. *Morals and Ethics.* New Delhi: Ambassador Press, n.d.

Dryden, Windy. Jill Mytton, *Four Approaches to Counselling Psychotherapy*. London: Routledge, 2005.

Duncan, David (Ed.) *Drug and the whole Person,* New York : John Wiley and Sons, 1982.

Earle, Nick. *What's Wrong with the Church*? Hamondsworth: Penguin Books, 1961.

Edwards, J. F. *Liquor and Opium in India*. London: Joint Overseas Temperance and Social Welfare Committee. 1929.

Ellis, Joe S. *The Church on Purpose.* Cincinnati: Standard Publishing, 1982.

Ellul, Jacques. The Theological Foundation of Law. London: Student Christian Movement, 1961.

Flynn, Lesslie B. *Great Church Fights.* Wheaton: Victor Books, 1976.

Foster, Greg. *Christian Ethics in Old Testament*, Series No. 35. Bramcote : Grove, 1980.

________ . *Cultural Patterns and Moral Laws*, Series No.17. Bramcote: Grove Books, 1977.

Fuchs, Josef S. J. *Personal Responsibility and Christian Morality.* Washington DC: George Town University Press, 1983.

Garvis, Alfred E. Can We still Follow Jesus? London: Cassell and Co. Ltd., 1913.

Geisler, Norman L. *Ethics*. Grand Rapids: Academic Books Zondervan. 1971.

Getz, Gene A. *Sharpening the Focus of the Church*. Chicago: Moody Press, 1981.

Glover, Robert Hall. *The Bible Basis of Missions*, Los Angeles: Bible House of Los Angeles. 1946.

Grimer, Howard. *The Church Redemptive*. New York: Abingdon Press, 1958.

Guinness, OS. *The Dust of Death*, Downers Grove : IVP, 1973.

Hardman, Peter G. And Eric Jay, *Probe 2, Drugs*. London: Pergamon Press Ltd., 1965.

Harrison, Earnest. *A Church Without God*. New York: J B Lippincott Co., 1967.

Harms, Ernest (Ed.) *Drug Addiction in Youth*. London Pergamon Press Ltd., 1965.

Hofmann, Frederick G. *A Handbook on Drug and Alcohol Abuse*. New York: Oxford University Press, 1983.

Hopkins, E.W. *Ethics of India*. London : Oxford University Press, 1924.

Hughes, Philip E. *Christian Ethics in Secular Society*. Grand Rapids: Baker Book House, 1984.

Jacob, Edmond. *Theology of the Old Testament*. New York: Harper and Row, 1958.

Jones, Richard Nelson., *Basic Counselling Skills: A Helpers Manual*. London: Sage Publications, 2011.

_________ ., *Cognitive Humanistic Therapy*, New Delhi: Sage Publications, 2004.

_________ ., *Essential Counselling and Therapy Skills*. New Delhi: Sage Publications, 2002.

_________ ., *Practical Counselling and Helping Skills*, New Delhi: Sage Publications, 2005.

________., *Six Key approaches to Counselling and Therapy*. London: Continuum, 2000.

Kaiser, Walter C. Jr. *Toward Old Testament Ethics*. Grand Rapids: Academic Books, Zondervan, 1983.

Kaye, Bruce. *Using the Bible in Ethics*, Series No.13. Bramcote: Grove Books, 1979.

Kasler, Jay. *Paremts and Teenagers*. Wheaton: Victor Books, 1984.

Lawton, Kenneth J. (ed.) *The Christian Response to Alcohol and Drug Problems*. Bangalore: Ecumenical Christian Centre, Inc., 1983.

Leech, Kenneth. *A Practical Guide to the Drug Scene*. London: Sheldon Press, 1974.

Linde Smith, Alfred R. *Addiction and Opiates*. Chicago: Aldine Publishing Co., 1970.

Littauer, Florence. *Personality Plus*. New Jersey: Fleming H. Revell Co., 1983.

Lobo, Benjamin P. *The Answers to Drug Addiction*. Bombay: Joseph Fernandes Printers, 1986.

Lohfink, Gerhard. *Jesus and Community*. London: SPCK, 1985.

Louria, Donald B. *Overcoming Drugs*. New York: McGraw-Hill Book Co., 1971.

McGavran, Donald. *Understanding Church Growth*. Madras: Evangelical Literature Service, 1982.

Marshall, H. S. *Portrait of the Early Church*. London: SPCK, 1952.

Marshall, Catherine. *The Helper*. Waco: Chosen Books, 1978.

Martin, William R. *Drug Addiction II*. Berlin: Springer Verlag, 1977.

Merchant, Yusuf A. *Brown Sugar Addiction*. Bombay: St. Marthoma Day Care Centre, 1987.

Metzger, Will. *Tell the Truth*. Downers Grove: InterVarsity Christian Fellowship, 1981.

Miller, Samule H. *The Life of the Church*. New York : Harper and Brothers, 1953.

Morton, T Ralph, *Community of Faith*. New York: A Haddman House Book, Association Press, 1954.

Murray, John. *Collected Writings. Vol. 2. Select Lectures in Systematic Theology*. London: Banner of Truth Trust.

________ . *Principles of Conduct*. Grand Rapids: Wm. B. Eerdmans, 1984.

Newbigin, Lesslie. *The Open Secret*., Grand Rapids: Wm.B. Eerdmans Co., 1983.

Niebuhr, H Richard. *The Purpose of the Church and Its Ministry*. London: Harper and Row, 1977.

Nygran, Anders. *Christ and His Church*. London: SPCK, 1957.

Oates, Wayne E. *The Christian Pastor*. Philadelphia: The Westminster, 1982.

O'Donnel, John A. *Narcotic Addiction*. New York: Harper & Row, 1966.

Olson, G. Keith. *Why Teenagers Act the Way They Do?* Loveland: Group Books, 1987.

O'Toole, Michael. *Drugs and Youth in India*. Goa: The OM Yeshu Niketan Society, 1987.

Palmer, E. H. *The Quran*. Vol. 9, Delhi: Motilal Banarsidas, 1977.

Pennenberg, Wolfhart. *The Church*. Philadelphia: The Westminster Press, 1983.

________ . *The Ethics*. Philadelphia: The Westminster Press. 1981.

Parrott, Leslie. *Building Todays Church*. Grand Rapids : Baker Book House, 1982.

Pascal, Blaise. "The Provincial letters, Pensee's Scientific Treaties." *Great Books of the Western World*. Chicago: Encyclopaedia Britannica Inc., 1952.

Peschke, C. Henry, *Christian Ethics*, Vol. I. Bangalore: Theological Publications in India, 1981.

Peters, George W. *A Biblical Theology of Mission*. Chicag: Moody Press, 1981.

Prashantham, B. J. *Indian Case Studies in Therapeutic Counselling*. Vellore: Christian Counselling Centre, 2002.

Radhakrishna, S. *The Hindu View of Life*, London: George Allen & Unwin. 1963.

Raines, Robert A. *New Life in the Church*. New York: Harper and Row, 1961.

Rogers, Arthus Kenyon. *The Theory of Ethics*. New York: The Macmillan Co., 1922.

Rudnick, Milton L. *Christian Ethics for Today*. Grand Rapids: Baker Book House, 1979.

Samuel, Vinay & Chris Sugden (Ed.) *The Church in Response to Human Need*, Grand Rapids: Wm B Eerdmans, 1987.

Schiff, L. M. *The Christian in Society*. Mysore: The Christian Literature Society, 1960.

Shriver, Donald W.Jr. *The Gospel, the Church and the Social Change*. Madras: CLS, 1980.

Sider, Ronald J. *Toward a Theology of Social Change*. Exeter: The Paternoster, 1981.

Singer K. *The Prognosis of Narcotic Addiction*. London: Butterworths. 1975.

Smedes, Lewis. *Mere Morality*. Grand Rapids: Wm. B. Eerdmans, 1983.

Speer, Robert E. *A Young Man's Question*. New York: The Westminster Press, 1903.

Stott, John R. W. *Christian Mission in the Modern World*. Bombay: Gospel Literature Service, 1978.

__________. *Issues Facing Christians Today*. Bombay: Gospel Literature Service, 1987.

Sturt, Henry, *Human Value*. Cambridge: University Press, 1923.

Telang, Kashinath T. *The Bhagavad Gita*. Delhi: Motiala Banarsidass, 1983.

Thakur, Shivesh Chandra. *Christian and Hindu Ethics*. London: George Allen & Unwin Ltd., 1969.

Trueblood, Elton. *The Life We Prize*. Waco: World Books, 1972.

Unknown Christian. *How to Live the Victorious Life*. Grand Rapids: Zondervan, 1962.

Virgo, Leslie IEd.) *First Aid in Pastoral Care*. Edinburgh: T&T Clark Ltd., 1987.

Ward, Leo R. *Ethic: A College Text*. London: Harper & Row, 1965.

Warren, Max. *Perspectives in Mission*. London: Hodder & Stoughton, 1964.

________ . *The Christian Imperatives*. London: SCM, 1955.

Wead, Douglas. *The Compassionate Touch*. Carol Stream: Creation House. 1977.

Webber, Robert R. *The Church in the World.* Grand Rapids: Academic Books, Zondervan, 1986.

Wells, Brain. *Psychedelic Drugs*. n. p: Penguin, 1973.

Woods, Eric. *The Moral Maze*: Series No. 33. Bramcote: Grove Books, 1980.

Woods, G. P. *A Defence of Theological Ethics*. Cambridge: University Press, 1966.

Woodward, David Brainerd. *God, Man and Missions*. Glendale: Gospel Light Publication, 1964.

Worthington, Everett L. *How to Help the Hurting*. Downers Grove: IVP, 1985.

Wright, Christopher, J. H. *An Eye for an Eye: The Place of O.T. Ethics Today.* Downers Grove: IVP, 1983.

________ . *Living as the People of God*. Downers Grove: IVP, 1983.

________ . *The Use of the Bible in Social Ethics*. Bramcote: Grove Books, 1983.

Yancey, Philip and Tim Stafford. *Unhappy Secrets of the Christian Life*. Grand Rapids: Zondervan, 1978.